RUGBY L
A PEOPLE'S

RUGBY LEAGUE
A PEOPLE'S HISTORY

Tony Collins

Scratching Shed Publishing Ltd

Typeset in Warnock Pro Semi Bold and Palatino
Printed and bound in the United Kingdom by
Page Bros (Norwich) Ltd
Mile Cross Lane, Norwich, Norfolk NR6 6SA
Telephone 01603 778800

Page
Bros
Group

'I say with Mark Twain's bold, bad boy, that we glory in the sentence of outlawry pronounced on us, as freeing us from the tyrannical bondage of the English Union.'
– 'Northern Union supporter'
Yorkshire Post, 21 September 1895.

Contents

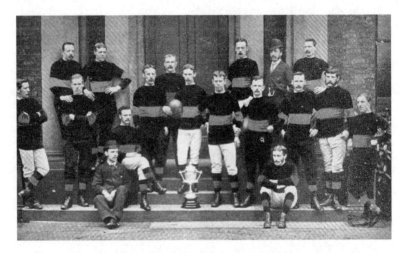

Rugby's first great side: The Wakefield Trinity team that appeared in five of the first six Yorkshire Cup finals – Teddy Bartram is standing, far right.

1
•

In the Beginning was Rugby...

'[Rugby] Football in the North of England ... has made
great strides during the past season, and in addition
to Manchester, Liverpool, Preston, Huddersfield,
Leeds, etc, etc, there are many clubs less widely known
in Yorkshire and Lancashire which can turn out a
fifteen both strong in play and possessing a good
knowledge of the science of the game.'
                                    — The Football Annual, 1877.

William Webb Ellis did not invent rugby.

No-one did.

The roots of rugby league, along with those of rugby
union, American football and even Australian Rules, can be
found in the rules of the game played at Rugby School in the
1800s. But the distinctive feature of rugby, picking up the ball
and running with it, was not the invention of an obscure
public schoolboy.

The truth is that for centuries, people throughout the
world have kicked, passed and carried a ball towards a goal.
You can see some of these games today, such as the traditional

Easter match still played in Workington, or the medieval Italian game *calcio*, played in Florence. These all became known as football.

None of these versions stopped people from handling the ball, as soccer does today. After all, it's as natural to pick up a ball as it is to kick it. The basic features of rugby have been around as long as people have selected two teams and tried to score against their opponents.

Soccer, with its refusal to allow outfield players to handle the ball, is the exception to this rule.

*****

These types of football game had been played in and around the town of Rugby long before its prestigious public school began playing. But when Thomas Hughes's *Tom Brown's Schooldays* became a bestselling novel in 1857, its depiction of a rugby match at the school meant that the game instantly became fashionable and was taken up by thousands of players across Britain.

Over the next decade and half, rugby's popularity grew so much that at the start of 1871 *Bell's Life*, Britain's leading sports weekly, reported that since the formation of the Football Association in 1863, '...every year has increased the superiority in point of numbers and popularity of the rugby clubs over those who are subject to the rule of the Association'. January 1871 also saw clubs in the south-east come together to form the Rugby Football Union (RFU), partly in order to counter the Football Association, but also to draw up a set of rules that could be used by the growing number of rugby clubs around the country.

By 1875, the RFU was strong enough to arrange annual internationals against Scotland and Ireland, hold an annual

North versus South match, and increase its membership five-fold to 113 clubs, 21 of them in the North of England. The first clubs in the north were formed in Liverpool and Manchester by former pupils of elite private schools such as Rugby and Eton, but other clubs were soon created by young men who had also been educated at local private schools, such as Bradford (1863), Leeds (1864) and Hull (1865).

Local rivalry between these clubs became infectious. 'We saw reports in the papers of football matches being played at Leeds, Bradford and elsewhere, and we thought that Halifax ought to have a club also,' was how Halifax's Sam Duckitt described his motivation for forming the club in 1873. The previous year Wigan F.C. had been formed, under the patronage of the mayor, in order to play matches against other towns. After six weeks' practice, they took to the field against Warrington. Four years later, Oldham F.C. was founded in similar circumstances. The rugby code of football was so popular in the north that it was simply referred as 'football'.

The 1870s saw numerous other clubs formed to represent their towns, often led by the sons of local textiles manufacturers, among them Brighouse, Dewsbury, Halifax, Rochdale, Swinton and Skipton. By 1875, at least 32 towns and cities in Lancashire and Yorkshire had a rugby-playing football club boasting their town's name, alongside dozens of other sides representing junior teams, local districts, or church organisations.

These clubs were formed simply to play matches against each other, with no thoughts of attracting spectators. But especially after the 1874 Factory Act, which reduced the working week from six days to five-and-a-half by forcing factories to close at 1pm on Saturday, rugby matches began to attract spectators. Just three years after its formation,

Wakefield Trinity noted in 1876 that 'the interest taken in the club by the public of Wakefield is something extraordinary' and recorded a profit of thirty-one shillings, despite the club not yet charging for admission to games.

They were not alone. For major games, crowds of 2,000 people were not unusual. Interest rose further after 1876 when the RFU reduced the size of teams from 20 to fifteen per side, and the game began to open up and become more attractive.

In 1877 the *Football Annual* reported that 'Football in the North of England ... has made great strides during the past season, and in addition to Manchester, Liverpool, Preston, Huddersfield, Leeds, etc, etc, there are many clubs less widely known in Yorkshire and Lancashire which can turn out a fifteen both strong in play and possessing a good knowledge of the science of the game.'

In Yorkshire, the game was boosted by the creation of the Yorkshire County Football Club (YCFC) in 1874. Unlike Lancashire, where the organisation of rugby was firmly in the hands of the patrician Manchester and Liverpool clubs, the YCFC comprised representatives of Bradford, Huddersfield, Hull, Leeds and York. Arthur Hudson, the son of a Leeds woollen manufacturer, joined the committee a year or so later and made a proposal which would revolutionise rugby: to start a knock-out cup competition for the leading teams in Yorkshire. So in December 1877, sixteen teams were invited to play for the Yorkshire Challenge Cup.

It began with a bang.

A massive crowd of 8,000 people packed into Halifax's Hanson Lane ground to see the local side defeat Wakefield F.C. in the first round. A week later, 500 Halifax supporters went by special train to Wakefield to watch their team overcome Wakefield Trinity. When Hull played

Heckmondwike in the second round, Hull's William Hutchinson recalled: '...there was so much excitement over the match among the local public that we really were fortunate in getting away from the ground without having to fight our way out... the spectators swarmed all about the field and there was a scene that up to that time we had not been accustomed to.' Unfortunately, heavy snow caused the final between Halifax and York to be switched from Huddersfield to Holbeck in Leeds, where a disappointing crowd of 3,000 saw Halifax carry off the trophy.

The next season was even more successful when 20 teams entered and an unprecedented 10,000 people crammed into Wakefield Trinity's Belle Vue to see them defeat Halifax. 12,000 spectators watched Trinity lift the cup in the final at Halifax's Thrum Hall when Kirkstall were defeated. As soon as the news of Trinity's victory was received in their home town: '...the Parish Church bells began to ring in honour of the event. On the arrival at Wakefield of the special train, the victors were met by the Parish Church Association band and an immense concourse of people, and marched from the station to the Woolpacks Inn, the cheering in the streets being again and again renewed.'

Rugby was now no longer confined to well-to-do young men. The Yorkshire Cup opened the door to new players, new spectators and new playing methods. The *Yorkshireman* magazine explained that Halifax's victory in the first final led to 'clubs springing up like mushrooms on every side. People saw that the "blue and whites", after a paltry connection with the sport of three years standing, had earned so much distinction, and why shouldn't they succeed in the same manner?'

The Yorkshire Cup brought football and civic pride together: 'I copt t'fooitball fever at t'same time as monny a hundred moor did – when t'Yorkshire Cup wor first laiked for thirteen year sin, and what's moor – or less, if owt – I've hed it ivver sin,' was how one fan summed up the impact of the cup.

And the importance of the cup to team and town meant that clubs began to search for good players who could help them win it. When Wakefield Trinity's star half-back Rufus Ward joined Halifax in the winter of 1877, many suspected he had been offered an 'inducement' to switch clubs, known as 'kidnapping':

> Well Rufus hed nobbut nicely gotten browt aht afoor he fell aht wi' some o' t'Trinity chaps an' fell in wi' Halifax. Nah doan't be sa sharp. Ah didn't say 'at t'Cup started t'kidnapping bizness. Only this is t'fust case 'at I knaw, an' it wor just ta help Halifax ta win t'Cup t'fust time, like. Two an' two, ye knaw – fower.

By 1884 it was estimated that over 100,000 people watched the Yorkshire Cup's first round matches, with the Dewsbury versus Wakefield Trinity game attracting more than 15,000 spectators. A few weeks later the *Dewsbury Reporter* pointed out that the Blackburn Rovers v Queen's Park 1884 FA Cup final drew only 10,000, while 15,000 had gathered at Halifax to see Bradford's semi-final defeat of Batley: 'It will be noticed that the Yorkshire monster attendances are far in excess of those of the metropolis with its millions of inhabitants'. Until the late 1880s, the Yorkshire Cup final often had a higher attendance than the soccer decider. In 1887, Arthur Hudson calculated that 350,000 people watched that year's 63 Yorkshire Cup ties. A sizeable portion of these spectators were women, who as far back as the first Yorkshire versus Lancashire game in 1870 had been going to matches in significant numbers.

But the Lancashire rugby authorities resisted the calls to start a Lancashire Cup, because they followed the lead of the RFU, which opposed cup competitions and refused to start a national rugby equivalent of the FA Cup. This restricted rugby's growth in Lancashire – and helped soccer – as can be seen by the fact that in 1890 the Yorkshire Rugby Union had 198 affiliated clubs but the Lancashire Rugby Union never had more than 50 members. Crowds in Lancashire were therefore slower to take off, but their rapid growth can be seen in the money taken by Salford and Warrington during the mid-1880s. In 1883, Salford's gate receipts were £160, which ballooned to £570 four years later. Warrington's growth was even more remarkable, rising from just £34 to slightly more than £1,234 in the same period, helped by the start of the West Lancashire and Border Towns cup competition in 1886.

This was Lancashire's nearest equivalent to the Yorkshire Cup. The key teams – Wigan were the most northerly club, while the other eleven came from the Merseyside area, including St Helens, Warrington and Widnes – were forced into action by the rise of soccer and the popularity of its cup competitions, so the West Lancs Cup was started to encourage local rugby rivalries. In 1889 a league competition also began. The South East Lancashire Rugby Union was formed in 1884 by clubs in the Manchester area district and other local cups followed. Around 18,000 people watched the final of the Wigan Challenge Cup in 1886; 16 sides contested the first Rochdale Charity Cup in 1887 and the following year it was estimated that 10,000 people watched the cup final.

But this massive influx of working-class players and

spectators into rugby was viewed suspiciously by the RFU. Not only were they wary of the enthusiastic crowds – London rugby journalist BF Robinson described them as 'howling mobs that crowd the circular stands of some Yorkshire coliseum' – they did not like the growing success of northern teams composed of miners, dockers and factory workers. In 1889, the RFU started a County Championship tournament which in its first eight years was won seven times by Yorkshire and once by Lancashire.

As one writer put it in 1892:

> The majority of Yorkshire fifteens are composed of working men, who have only adopted football in recent years, and have received no school education in the art. The majority of members of London clubs have played it all their lives, yet when the two meet there is only one in it - the Yorkshireman.

To the men who led the RFU, it seemed like control of rugby was slipping out of their hands.

2

•

Rugby's Great Split

'If the blind enthusiasts of working men's clubs insist on introducing professionalism, there can be but one result – disunion... And if this black day comes, which I hope it never will, it will be the duty of the Rugby Union to see that the division of classes dates from the dawn of professionalism.'
– Arthur Budd, former RFU president, 1892.

If you asked any northern rugby fan in the early 1880s who was the best three-quarter in England, they would reply 'Teddy' Bartram. Tall, fast and elegant, he was the linchpin of the Wakefield Trinity side that played in five successive Yorkshire Cup finals, winning three. He played 16 times for Yorkshire and was the most gifted back in the county before the rise of Dewsbury's Dicky Lockwood. Yet he was never selected for England.

Born in Leeds in 1857, Charles Edward Bartram was a naturally-gifted sportsman, who as a cricket professional would later play 23 matches for Northumberland in cricket's

Minor Counties Championship. He began playing rugby as a centre-threequarter for Harrogate in the 1870s and in 1878 produced a stunning display against Wakefield Trinity, who promised to take care of travelling expenses if he transferred to them. In 1881, he was offered a job as Trinity's assistant secretary – but there was no position of 'assistant secretary'; it was a fiction to disguise the fact he was being paid to play. He agreed, and became rugby's first-ever professional player.

Teddy was never picked by the RFU for England because, as Oxford University and England full-back Harry Tristram pointed out, 'his position was not entirely that of an amateur and the rugby union did not want to raise the question of professionalism'. Eventually, he would become one of the many victims of the RFU's amateur regulations and was banned from rugby for life in 1889 after being found guilty of receiving a loan from the club.

*****

Bartram was an electrical engineer and symbolised the problem the RFU had with the huge influx of working-class players in the sport, as the *Yorkshire Post* argued:

> Why are so few public school men and clergymen found in our leading fifteens? ... They do not care to be hooted and yelled at as part and parcel of a sixpenny show or to meet and associate with men who care nothing for the game other than as a means to an end. We have nothing to say against the mechanic, the artisan or the labourer, who as long as they indulge in the game for sport and not for profit, are an ornament to the game.

The rise of the mechanic, artisan and labourer in rugby made the RFU worry that their code would go the same way as professional soccer. The FA Cup had traditionally been dominated by teams of former public schoolboys, such as the Old Etonians and the Wanderers. But in the 1884-85 season the FA legalised professionalism, and after 1885 no team of privately-educated players ever again played in the FA Cup final.

Rugby's leaders worried this would also be their fate. Arthur Budd, soon to become president of the RFU, feared professionalism in rugby would mean that the middle-class amateur would become subordinate to the working-class professional, turning the British class system upside down. He called for 'no mercy but iron rigour' in order to 'throttle the hydra' of the 'working man professional'.

Harry Garnett, the Bradford paper-mill owner who became Yorkshire's first president of the RFU, said bluntly: 'If working men desired to play football, they should pay for it themselves, as they would have to do with any other pastime'.

So in 1886, the RFU turned in the opposite direction to the FA and declared rugby would now be a purely amateur sport. Players could not be paid money nor receive any other reward for playing the game. Any player found guilty of breaking the amateur rules would be suspended or banned from the sport. The game was about to be torn apart.

One player targeted for investigation by the rugby authorities was Dicky Lockwood, arguably England's greatest player of the 1880s and 1890s. Born in Crigglestone, near Wakefield, Dicky made his debut as a right wing three-quarter for Dewsbury aged 16 in 1884, rapidly establishing himself as a star of the game. Nicknamed 'the Little Tyke' and 'Little Dick, the World's Wonder', partly because of his age and also because of his diminutive stature – he was only five feet, four inches tall – Dicky played for Yorkshire and England at the age of 19. Fast, strong and a smart tactician, he introduced the Welsh four three-quarter system into the Yorkshire county team and was famed for his uncanny ability to be in the right place at the right time.

He worked as a manual labourer and in 1889 transferred to Heckmondwike, a club that had built a winning team by offering under-the-counter payments and jobs in the booming local textile factories.

Dicky was investigated twice for professionalism by the rugby authorities but there was never enough evidence to convict him. When he was found not guilty, the local newspaper reported how: '...hundreds of people collected in Heckmondwike market place and its approaches, and the news of his acquittal was received with an outburst of cheering, the gathering in all respects resembling those witnessed at an exciting political election.' Nevertheless, he was so talented that between 1887 and 1894 he was an automatic choice for England and even captained England in 1894. But the tension between Dicky and the game's leaders epitomised the relationship between the supporters of amateurism who ran the game and working class players who had come to dominate its playing: 'Dicky doesn't sport sufficient collar and cuff for the somewhat fastidious members of the committee,' it was reported in 1891.

The investigations into players like Lockwood showed how the imposition of amateurism on rugby had created an atmosphere of paranoia in the North.

An accusation that a player had been paid or a club was paying players could lead to the suspension of star men or cancellation of fixtures, causing the loss of significant amounts of gate money. Amateurism threatened to cripple rugby in Lancashire and Yorkshire, as one player pointed out in 1891:

> To carry out amateurism to its logical conclusion would be to depopularise the game and make it the selfish possession of the silver-spooned classes. Moreover, it would deprive the pastime of its ablest and most numerous exponents, who are essentially the working men of the North, and of its most enthusiastic supporters, who are undoubtedly the wage-earning classes.

Discontent about the direction rugby was taking led to Yorkshire clubs starting a campaign for players to be paid for time they had to take off work to play the game, known as 'broken-time' payments. In April 1891 Yorkshire Rugby Union secretary James Miller, of Leeds, outlined the case for broken-time payments:

> Rugby is no longer the pastime of the public schools and the leisured classes alone; it has become the sport of the masses – of the wage-earning classes in our great manufacturing centres. ... it is unreasonable to expect the same 'amateurism' from the wage-earning classes as from public school men. It is unfair to expect working men to break time to play football without their being remunerated.

Although the Northern clubs felt that broken-time payments might be accepted as a compromise, the RFU simply refused. It was amateurism or split. Writing in the 1892 *Athletic News Annual* RFU committee member, Huddersfield's Reverend

Frank Marshall, declared: 'It is far preferable to have two bodies, one amateur and the other professional, than to have the methods of the Football Association imitated by the Rugby Union.'

Even so, the supporters of broken-time payments were confident they could win a majority of RFU clubs to support the concept, and so the Yorkshire clubs decided to put the proposal to the vote at the RFU's annual general meeting in September 1893. They were backed by the Lancashire Rugby Union, which voted to support the motion because 'the game is both supported and played extensively by the working classes, and their players feel as keenly as ours the pinch of the shoe in the loss of broken time'.

The meeting was held at the plush Westminster Palace Hotel in London. Yorkshire's James Miller proposed the resolution that 'players be allowed compensation for bona-fide loss of time.' He argued that rugby no longer belonged to the public schools and universities, and that the RFU did working-class players an injustice. 'These men were constantly called upon to lose their wages in order to play for their county or their club and at the same time they were debarred from recompense for the loss of time involved. Why should not the working man be able to play the game on level terms with the gentleman?'

He described how Harry Bradshaw, Bramley's star forward, who worked at Newlay Dyeworks in Leeds, had played for England against Ireland in Dublin in February, but lost three days' pay to travel to and from the match. Miller said this was not fair: 'The game should be played as a sport and not as a source of income, but it did not mean that these players should play it at a loss. If it was legitimate to refund expenses, why not refund wages lost?'

After an extensive debate, the motion to legalise

broken-time payments was lost by 282 votes to 136. Straight after the meeting the RFU changed its constitution to allow only clubs 'entirely composed of amateurs' to be members. Supporters of broken-time responded with outrage. The *Yorkshireman* said: 'We have at last been boldly told the truth ... if a man cannot afford to play he has no right to; that Rugby football is a game for the classes and, in effect, that the masses are neither more nor less than intruders.'

Rugby was now in a state of open civil war, and the *Yorkshire Owl* magazine warned prophetically that: 'The English Rugby Union ... will never stand professionalism in the game, whatever name it is cloaked under ... It would have to sacrifice many fine exponents of the game doubtless, but it would not hesitate. It would lose a good many international games, but it would still not hesitate'. Shortly afterwards, Huddersfield were found guilty of professionalism and suspended until 1894 after allegedly offering John Forsyth and George Boak, two players from Cummerdale Hornets in Cumberland, money and jobs at the Reed, Holliday chemical works if they moved to Fartown.

The war soon moved across the Pennines. At the start of the 1894-95 season the Lancashire Rugby Union suspended Leigh for ten weeks for illegally paying and providing board and lodgings to two Welsh players, Dai Fitzgerald and Charlie Wilding. As well as being suspended, the club was automatically placed at the bottom of Lancashire rugby's first division, and banned from charging spectators at any rearranged games when the period ended. Three weeks later, Salford were charged with offering Radcliffe's Joe Smith 25 shillings a week to transfer to them. They received the same punishment as Leigh. On 13 November, Wigan also suffered the same fate when they too were found guilty of professionalism.

Faced with being picked off one-by-one by the RFU, 18 clubs met at the George Hotel in Huddersfield on 30 January 1895 to create the 'Lancashire and Yorkshire Rugby Football Union of Senior Clubs'. The new organisation planned to organise an annual challenge match between the Lancashire and Yorkshire club champions, and control transfers between member clubs. Secretly, the clubs also agreed to support each other if they were suspended or expelled by the RFU.

As the civil war escalated, it was complicated by a dispute over automatic promotion and relegation. The Yorkshire Senior Competition – the league created in 1892 for the top ten Yorkshire clubs – was a self-elected body with no promotion or relegation. But at the end of the 1893-94 season, the rugby union authorities tried to force the Senior Competition to accept a play-off between its bottom club and the winner of the Second Competition, as division two was called.

However, the Senior Competition insisted that the bottom club could be excused from the play-off match if there were 'unforeseen circumstances'. This was to protect clubs which finished at the bottom because they had been suspended for professionalism, as happened to Huddersfield, Leigh, Salford and Wigan. Unable to reach a compromise, in July 1895 the Yorkshire Senior Competition clubs and the first division Lancashire clubs, except Salford and Swinton, resigned from their county rugby unions.

Following this skirmish, the decisive battle broke out on 12 August 1895 when the RFU announced that its September annual general meeting would introduce a new rule which meant any club, player or official accused of professionalism would be suspended until they could prove their innocence. It was the RFU's final nail in the coffin of compromise.

In response, at 6.30 pm on Thursday, 29 August 1895 at the George Hotel in the centre of Huddersfield – chosen because it was almost equidistant between Widnes in the west and Hull in the east – representatives of Batley, Bradford, Brighouse Rangers, Broughton Rangers, Dewsbury, Halifax, Huddersfield, Hull, Hunslet, Leeds, Leigh, Liversedge, Manningham, Oldham, Rochdale Hornets, St Helens, Tyldesley, Wakefield Trinity, Warrington, Widnes and Wigan met. They quickly and unanimously voted for a resolution that stated, 'That the clubs here represented decide to form a Northern Rugby Football Union, and pledge themselves to push forward, without delay, its establishment on the principle of payment for bona-fide broken-time only.' It was a declaration of principle – every rugby player would now be able to play the game to the fullest extent of their talent and ability, regardless of their occupation, background or status. Equality of opportunity was at the very core of the new organisation.

Although not present at the George Hotel, Stockport were asked to join. All the clubs except Dewsbury, whose committee had not had time to discuss the matter, handed their letters of resignation from the RFU to Oldham's Joseph Platt, who had been elected acting secretary, to send to his RFU counterpart Rowland Hill. The Northern Union had been born – and rugby would never be the same.

The Northern Union (NU) had overwhelming support from players and supporters. Newspapers reported that players in Huddersfield 'naturally champion the Northern Union and a very large section of spectators of matches take the same side'. At Broughton Rangers, the motion to join the NU was moved by the club captain and carried unanimously. Hunslet, St Helens, Manningham, Hull and Leigh were similarly united. Although they went to the George Hotel meeting, Dewsbury decided not join the NU and stayed loyal to the RFU. It was not a popular decision. A local journalist reported that '...there wasn't a single supporter who wouldn't say "Let us have the Northern Union and the sooner the better".'

The summer of 1896 saw Lancashire's remaining big clubs join the NU. In April 1896, Salford held a special meeting to discuss joining the NU where only three people opposed the switch. Rochdale St Clements, Radcliffe, Werneth, Morecambe and many others followed suit that summer. Most of Warrington's local clubs went at the same time, as did around 50 clubs which formed the Oldham Junior Rugby League.

At the same time in Yorkshire most of the clubs in the first division of Yorkshire rugby union's leagues decamped to the NU. Leeds Parish Church, that season's champions, had only five members vote against their switch of allegiance. In June 1897, Hull KR, that year's Yorkshire cup and league champions, also abandoned rugby union. In 1899, Hebden Bridge, Ossett, Kirkstall and Alverthorpe flew the nest and, in the summer of 1900, Keighley, Otley and Bingley decided that 'the interest has gone out of rugby union' and joined the NU. Morley and Otley – two of Yorkshire's most important rugby union clubs – owe their origins to the aftermath of 1895. The original Morley outfit joined the NU in May 1897. Two months later, rugby union supporters founded the new 'Morley English Rugby Football Club', the forerunner of the present union club. The original Otley rugby club resigned from the RFU in 1900 and played rugby league for six seasons before disbanding due to financial problems. The current side was founded as a new rugby union club in 1907.

In the North West, Barrow – the region's leading club – voted unanimously to join the NU in April 1897. Ulverston, whose fans raised a petition in support of the NU, Millom, and most of the North West followed them in July. The loss of the north-west Lancashire clubs had a knock-on effect on those in Cumberland and Westmorland, and by January 1899 there was not a single rugby union club left in west Cumberland.

The idea that the split in 1895 was a 'breakaway' from rugby union underestimates the sheer scale of what happened in 1895. The heart and soul of rugby in the north went over to the NU. Its senior clubs were the strongest in England and its local amateur sides were at the core of rugby's appeal in Yorkshire, what is now Cumbria and large parts of Lancashire.

If the meeting at the George Hotel in 1895 signaled the birth of rugby league, the aftermath of the split showed that it was the Northern Union that continued the historic traditions that had made rugby the passion of countless men and women across the industrial north of England.

A joint soccer and rugby programme from 1899 for Manchester City,
Newton Heath, Broughton Rangers and Salford matches

3

•

Best in t'Northern Union

'The executive committee of the Northern Union
cannot be called a conservative body. Every season it
has evinced a desire to amend the rules of the game in
accordance with the ideas of the progressives.'
— *Athletic News Football Annual*, 1906.

Albert Goldthorpe made his debut for Hunslet in October 1888 at full-back, aged just 16. He was, reported the *Leeds Mercury*, '...properly put to the test and came through the ordeal with flying colours.' He soon moved into the centres and became known as one of the game's greatest drop-kickers.

He was selected to play for Yorkshire aged 20, when the county swept all before it and, in 1892, was in the Yorkshire team that defeated a full-strength England national side. He played his last match, aged 40, in 1911 – a career of over 22 years at the top of both rugby league and rugby union.

When the Northern Union was created, Goldthorpe became an even greater player. He was the first to score 100

goals in a season and, at the age of 36, captained Hunslet to
All Four Cups in 1908, the first side ever to win the Grand
Slam of Challenge Cup, Championship, County Cup and
County League. Based on its 'Terrible Six' forward pack and
boasting great three-quarters like Fred Farrar, 'the Farsley
Flyer', and the legendary Billy Batten, this was the first truly
great team in rugby league history.

But Goldthorpe represented much more than statistics.
He organised benefit matches to raise funds for striking
workers and, in 1904, the Leeds & District Schoolboys Trophy
was named after him, in tribute to the tremendous work he
had put into the sport. 'Ahr Albert' as he was known, became
a symbol of Hunslet, its community, and of rugby league
itself.

Goldthorpe and his fellow players were the inspiration
for the saying 'T best in t'Northern Union' which began to be
used across the north of England before World War One. The
phrase meant that something was of the highest quality,
reflecting the belief that the best in the Northern Union was
the best that existed.

Just as Goldthorpe was more than just a sporting
celebrity, rugby league was about more than merely sport.

*****

As soon as it was created, the Northern Union began to bring
rugby into the modern age.

A single league for all professional clubs was
immediately established and the Challenge Cup began as
rugby's answer to the FA Cup the following season.

Most significantly, the Northern Union changed the
way rugby was played. Under the RFU's first rules of rugby,
teams were 20-a-side, consisting usually of two full-backs,

two half-backs, one three-quarter, and fifteen forwards. The scrum was the heart of the game, but it was nothing like today's scrums.

When brought down in a tackle, the ball-carrier was allowed to stand up, wait for both sets of forwards to gather around, and then put the ball down, shout 'Down' and the scrum began. The aim was not to heel the ball out but to drive it forward and scatter the opposing pack. Scrums often went on for minutes, while both packs tried to push their opponents back. Passing the ball was extremely rare.

This was not a game for spectators.

In 1875, *Bell's Life* asked: 'How much longer are we to be wearied by monotonous shoving matches?' In response, the RFU decided that international matches would be fifteen-a-side, and rugby at all levels quickly followed suit. The reduction meant fewer forwards and smaller scrums which no longer lasted for minutes. Now teams began to heel the ball deliberately, and the speed with which it left the scrum now offered the half-back the chance to pass the ball quickly out to his three-quarters or loose-forward.

In 1878, the RFU decided that a tackled player had to let go of the ball immediately. Forwards now had to keep up with the play, which opened up the field and created more opportunities for the backs. In those areas where rugby was now a mass spectator sport, new tactics emerged. Cardiff introduced the four three-quarter system in the mid-1880s and, in the north of England, the huge popularity of the Yorkshire Cup tournament propelled the game to new levels of tactical sophistication.

The bigger the crowds got, the more it became apparent that tries, rather than goals, were what spectators came to see. Originally, only goals counted in a rugby score; a try merely allowed the scorer to try to kick a goal. But pressure from northern clubs led to the RFU introducing a points system in 1886, awarding one point for a try and three for a goal. But it was a case one step forward, two steps back in 1889 when penalty goals became worth two points. In 1891, the value of a drop-goal was raised to four points.

Yet for most spectators, especially in Northern England and South Wales, the passing game and the scoring of tries were the essence of rugby, as one Yorkshire journalist argued:

> A try in the vast majority of instances is the most deserving point in the game, and calls for the greatest exertion on the part of the team as a whole. On the other hand, the responsibility of placing a goal is an individual responsibility.

In 1892, Yorkshire's James Miller praised rugby's move to fifteen-a-side in the previous generation but argued that it was time to go further: 'the game had now reached a period when another radical change must be considered, and that was the reduction of players from fifteen to thirteen.' Well before the creation of the Northern Union in 1895, an alternative roadmap for the future of rugby was being laid out.

Just two weeks after the formation of the Northern Union, Halifax and Leeds proposed moving to thirteen-a-side rugby, with Leeds committee member Harry Sewell arguing:

> We want to do away with that scrummaging, pushing and thrusting game, which is not rugby ... that is why I propose to abolish the line-out and reduce the number of forwards to six. The rugby public does not pay to see a lot of scrummaging.

In December 1895, Halifax's Joe Nicholl proposed to the NU that the game: '...should be played by thirteen players on each side, and to consist of six forwards, two half-backs, four three-quarters and one full-back'. But many felt this was too radical and Nicholl lost the vote by 18 to 9, and the NU continued to play a fifteen-a-side game.

The NU's hesitation cost it dearly. At the end of the first season, there were worries about the lack of tries scored, so in 1897 the value of all goals was reduced to two points, one less than a three-point try, firmly emphasising try scoring. The line-out was also abolished in 1897 and replaced by a 'punt-out' from touch, but that proved to be even more chaotic than the line-out, so a scrum was formed when the ball was kicked into touch.

In 1899, the NU got rid of the ruck and maul by ruling that when a tackled player could not release the ball, a scrum had to be formed. Although this tidied up the tackle it hugely increased the number of scrums – in 1902, Hunslet's match with Halifax had 110 scrums.

One solution was to reduce the number of forwards. In 1903, clubs voted 54 to 24 to make the game twelve-a-side, but the motion failed by just five votes to get the necessary three-quarters majority to go into the rule book. But twelve-a-side was popular and by 1905 it had been adopted by virtually every non-professional NU competition. The issue was debated again at the 1906 NU annual meeting. Whitehaven Recreation wanted twelve men, Warrington and Leigh proposed thirteen and St Helens even suggested fourteen. Finally, thirteen-a-side was adopted, 43 votes to 18.

To solve the problem of endless scrums, the meeting also decided to introduce the play-the-ball. Now, instead of a scrum being formed, a tackled player was allowed to stand up, put the ball down and play it with the foot, usually to a team-mate behind him. This was actually a variation of the original rugby union rule, when a tackled player had to stand up and put the ball down to start the scrum.

The introduction of thirteen-a-side teams and the play-the-ball marked the birth of modern rugby league, and the impact of these changes was felt instantly. Over 800 points were scored in the first two weeks of the 1906-07 season, a runaway record, and the *Athletic News* boldly declared: 'The New Rules Completely Vindicated.'

The Soccer Threat

The long delay in changing to thirteen-a-side hindered the game when it needed help most. The early 1900s were a testing time for the new Northern Union.

The league structure was constantly tinkered with, moving from one division, through a breakaway elite league, on to two divisions and eventually settling back into one division based on county fixtures. County cups were introduced in Lancashire and Yorkshire in 1905 to boost interest, and international rugby league began inauspiciously in 1904, when the Other Nationalities beat England, 9-3, at Wigan's Central Park in a twelve-a-side match.

The economic depression of the early 1900s also took a heavy toll, with founding Northern Union clubs such as Brighouse, Liversedge, Stockport and Tyldesley collapsing.

But the biggest threat came from soccer. By the mid-1890s, association football leagues had been established in most traditional rugby towns. Manchester and Liverpool, where rugby had dominated for a generation, had become hot-beds of the round-ball game and, across the north, soccer's growth in schools and communities was rapidly undermining the bedrock of rugby support.

In Yorkshire, the former rugby town of Barnsley had been swamped by association, and in December 1898 the Beckett Cup, the district rugby knock-out competition trophy, was handed to the local FA because there were no rugby teams left to play for it. In Hull, the decade after the 1895 split saw local soccer sides grow from just seven to 96. By 1904, there were 436 clubs affiliated to the West Yorkshire FA, at least four times the number of rugby ones in the area.

Soccer's appeal was not simply due to its more open style of play: in an era of national culture, soccer was a truly national sport. By 1906, the FA claimed over 7,500 affiliated clubs, roughly fifteen times the number of clubs playing league or union. As the *Leeds Mercury* pointed out in 1905:

> The public want a national game rather than a code peculiar to a circumscribed area. ... Thus, while the Northern Union has too limited an area to be really a great force, and the Rugby Union is to some extent discredited as a purely amateur combination and is weakened through the loss of the cream of the clubs of the North, the Association game is national in scope and influence, and is yearly becoming more powerful and more popular.

The Football League was keen to expand into rugby's northern industrial heartland. From 1900, rumours were rife in West Yorkshire that a professional soccer side in Leeds or Bradford would be asked to join the Football League. In 1901, Manningham, the Bradford club which had been the Northern Union's first ever league champions, told the West Yorkshire FA that 'we are doing all we possibly can to help the Association game'. It was not an accident that this coincided with a decline in the fortunes of the club, which saw them fall to the second tier of the league. Towards the end of 1902, the Manningham committee seems to have met the Football League and begun working with James Whyte, a Scottish journalist on the *Bradford Observer* and Charles Brunt, a soccer-loving local headmaster. Eventually, in May 1903, Manningham FC, one of the biggest names in rugby, was sensationally accepted into the Football League's Second Division without ever having played a single game of soccer.

Manningham's split reflected the changing nature of Britain. By 1900, it was no longer enough to be a big name in a county or a region. Bradford was one of the richest cities in Europe – not for nothing did T.S. Eliot talk about the silk hats on Bradford millionaires in his poem *The Waste Land* – and the businessmen who ran Manningham wanted their club to be a national phenomenon. In its first season, Bradford City, as Manningham renamed itself, doubled its crowds and income. But there was more to the switch than just cashflow. In the Northern Union, Manningham's committee saw itself as a middling club in a regional competition of a declining sport. Their civic pride could no longer be satisfied regionally; they wanted to be on the national stage.

Manningham's switch led other NU clubs to explore their options. At the end of the 1903-04 season, Holbeck NU club in south Leeds disbanded after losing a promotion play-off game. Six days later, the newly-formed Leeds City soccer club rented Holbeck's Elland Road ground and announced their intention it buy it for £5,000. It was not a coincidence that Holbeck chairman Joe Henry, a local businessman who would later become Lord Mayor of Leeds, was also chairman of the new Leeds City soccer club. In 1919, Leeds City became Leeds United.

The Northern Union was sufficiently worried by

soccer's threat that it decided in 1905: '...that no club shall be represented on the Union committee whose interest in football is not solely devoted to the Northern Union game.' But just three months later the *Yorkshire Post* ominously warned: '...indications are that before very long we shall have another association club [in Bradford].'

Bradford FC were the flagship of Yorkshire rugby's Golden Age of the 1880s and 1890s. The club had poured money into making its Park Avenue ground one of the best in England, but had struggled under the weight of its debt – by 1907, it had reached £7,000 – and they had already defaulted twice on annual payments. But there was another problem for the club. Manningham's switch to soccer had aroused jealousy among the Bradford committee, who were used to being the city's premier sports club. The fact the Northern Union had become a predominantly working-class sport also rankled with the club's patrician leaders. This sense of thwarted social status was captured by its official Harry Geldard when he said '...the downfall of the Northern Union game had been brought about by the election of men from small unknown places to represent the Union'.

But the Bradford committee was deeply split about what direction to take. In December 1906, it voted to leave the Northern Union unless it reverted back to rugby union rules. This was clearly impossible, but former captain Laurie Hickson approached the RFU about rejoining. He was told they would welcome the club back, but not its players, who were banned for life because they were professionals!

Three months later, newspapers reported that the Bradford committee wanted to join the Football League, but a special meeting of members again voted to return to rugby union. The committee ignored the meeting's decision and organised a postal ballot of members, which resulted in a majority for soccer. On 7 May, the club voted 18-2 to switch to soccer, 'recognising that association is the best paying game from a financial point of view'. Faced with the self-inflicted death of their rugby club, 300 supporters who remained loyal to the Northern Union met three weeks later to form Bradford Northern Union Football Club, and, not for the last time, kept the rugby flag flying in one of its historic cities.

The decision to switch to soccer didn't go as planned for Bradford. The Football League turned down its application to join. In a panic, the committee decided to join soccer's Southern League, where their nearest opponent was Northampton Town. It would be another year before they were finally admitted into the Football League. Ironically, in view of the club's desire to recapture its elite social standing of the 1880s, Bradford Park Avenue, as the soccer team became known, was forever destined to play second fiddle to its Bradford City rival.

Bradford's defection would be the last breach in the Northern Union. No other leading club would leave for soccer, although the Football League established professional clubs in Hull in 1905, Oldham in 1907, Huddersfield in 1910, and in Halifax and Rochdale in 1921. But the NU had stopped the defection of clubs and confidence began to return to the game. The next twelve months would see the start of a new era, one in which the Northern Union dramatically expanded in a way that no-one had previously imagined.

4
•

From Kiwis to Kangaroos

'Rugby League is a game for every class and all classes to play. It is not a caste game.'
— Horrie Miller, NSWRL secretary, 1921.

No-one symbolised the new era of rugby more than Harold Wagstaff. 'I am a Northern Union man all the way through', he proudly announced, in the opening sentence of his memoirs.

Born in Underbank, near Huddersfield, in 1891, he made his debut for Underbank Rangers aged 14 and in September 1906 scored their first try under the new thirteen-a-side rules. He then signed for Huddersfield aged 15 years and 175 days, the youngest-ever professional player at that time. A mere two years later he made his England debut against the 1908 Kangaroos. He became Huddersfield captain at 19 and then, aged 22, was made skipper of the national side.

His career reached its zenith as Huddersfield redefined rugby and became one of the greatest club sides in any code of football. The team melded together Welsh players such as

Johnny Rogers and Ben Gronow, the first man to kick-off in an international match at Twickenham, New Zealanders like centre Edgar Wrigley, and Australian stars including Glebe's Tommy Gleason and Newcastle's Paddy Walsh. Greatest of all was Eastern Suburbs' Albert Rosenfeld, who scored 366 tries in just 287 games while wearing Huddersfield's claret and gold. In the 1911-12 season he set a seemingly unbeatable record of 78 tries in a season, and then astonishingly topped it with 80 in 1913-14.

Huddersfield finished top of the Championship table every season between 1911 and 1915, won the Challenge Cup twice and the Yorkshire Cup three times. In 1914-15, they won every trophy available to them, losing only two games in the entire campaign. Their success was based on a fast, open game that made the fullest use of the opportunities provided by the Northern Union's new rules. Wagstaff and his men developed tactics – such as 'scientific obstruction', the 'standing pass' and a hostility to kicking the ball – which moved the game far beyond the static set-pieces of its origins.

Wagstaff's greatness was not just recognised at home. The Australians too held him in the highest esteem. He was the inspirational figure that led Britain to Ashes success in 1914, when he captained his side to victory in the deciding Third Test match, defeating Australia 14-6 in Sydney with just nine fit players on the pitch. Sid Deane, who played for North Sydney and later for Hull, said: 'Wagstaff was not only brilliant in attack and wonderful in defence but his leadership was a most important factor in the team's success.' Dinny Campbell of Eastern Suburbs and a future Leeds player, described him as 'the greatest tactician I ever played against. His personality was dynamic.'

As for his team-mates, the great forward Douglas Clark simply wrote in his diary after that historic win which, because of its rear-guard action became known as the 'Rorke's Drift' Test: 'Harold was the man!' Harold and his glorious side would become the benchmark against which all subsequent rugby league players and teams would be measured.

*****

Wagstaff was one of thousands of people who admired the New Zealand All Blacks' team which toured Britain in 1905. They won 34 out of 35 matches, scoring almost a thousand points against just 59, playing a dynamic running game that resembled Northern Union rugby more than traditional rugby union – on their entire tour, they kicked just four penalty goals. People flocked to see them and the tour made a profit of almost £9,000. Yet the players, lauded as national heroes when they returned to New Zealand, received only three shillings per day expenses. A newspaper report by an 'Original All Black', explained their frustrations:

> That they, the All Blacks, could scarcely raise £10 in the whole team on their return passage home to New Zealand is well known ... and it was generally admitted that the team were not well treated. Several were men of means, and could well afford the loss of time, but the majority were working men.

But the tour also showed many All Blacks that 'working-men' rugby players did not have to accept their poverty. They had seen how the Northern Union paid players and that it was possible to be rewarded for their rugby talent. What was more, the playing principles of Northern Union, even before the decisive rule changes of 1906, matched the open rugby philosophy of the New Zealand game.

The similarity between rugby in New Zealand and the Northern Union had been highlighted by George Stephenson, an Otago theatre owner, who played for Manningham before and after the 1895 split. In 1904 he wrote: 'New Zealand football is very similar to that of the North of England ... and resembles the present system of the professional game under the Northern Union.' It seems that at some point on the 1905 tour, All Black winger George Smith met with Northern Union officials. Smith had also been able to watch the NU during a 1902 trip to Britain to compete in an athletics tournament.

In March 1907, barely twelve months after the All Blacks had returned home, a letter arrived at the Northern Union's offices from Canterbury postal clerk Albert Baskerville. In it, Baskerville – who was a well-known player and author of *Modern Rugby Football*, a book that promoted open rugby – asked if the NU would support a tour to England by a professional All Black side later that year.

The NU accepted almost immediately. When the sensational news broke, Baskerville was declared persona non grata by the New Zealand Rugby Union (NZRU) and banned from all rugby grounds. The NZRU then demanded that every player selected for that year's North Island versus South Island match should sign a declaration stating they were amateurs and would inform the NZRU if approached by Baskerville. In England, Cecil Wray Palliser, the equivalent of the New Zealand ambassador to the UK, called Baskerville's team 'some kind of sensation to save the Northern Union. It is a phantom side.' It was a description gleefully seized upon by Baskerville's supporters.

But the spirit of rebellion among New Zealand rugby

players ran deep. Duncan MacGregor, the railway worker who scored four tries for the All Blacks against England in 1905, was one of the first to refuse to sign the NZRU's declaration. Of the 28 players who joined Baskerville, nine were All Blacks, including four from the 1905 tour. Every player who signed up for the 1907 tour knowingly sacrificed their rugby union career – the only certainty was they would be banned for life from playing it. The tour was truly a step into the unknown.

Baskerville's squad of professionals arrived in Leeds on the evening of 1 October 1907 and were astounded by the huge crowd and the jubilation which greeted them at Leeds railway station, as the *Yorkshire Post* reported:

> Bumper Wright, the New Zealand captain, called for "three cheers for the people of Leeds", which were followed by a stirring Maori war-cry and further cheering. The players were escorted to the Grand Central Hotel by the Hunslet charabanc and the Northern Union officials in carriages, together with the still cheering crowd. The crush was so dense in Boar Lane and Briggate as to cause the stoppage of traffic.

After a few days practising their new sport – amazingly, barely any players had seen, let alone played, rugby league – they undertook their first match, and went unbeaten in their first eight games, before losing to Wigan in front of 30,000 spectators at Central Park.

'Massa' Johnston, a 1905 union and 1907 league tourist who subsequently played for Wigan, later said: 'Charlie Mackrell, Duncan MacGregor and [my]self, had a good idea in 1905 what the union players were like, but not for one moment did we think we would meet such continuous opposition as we did in 1907 ... every match played in England was a test match ... No place for weaklings or one who has a habit of looking for the easy or flash stuff on a football field.'

By the time the tourists arrived back home ten months later in June 1908, they had won a three-match Test series against the Northern Union (as the national side was then called), been watched by over 300,000 people, and made a profit of more than five-and-a-half thousand pounds, which the players shared among themselves. Their impact on rugby in New Zealand was profound. By 1914, Auckland had 39 rugby league teams, the same as local union, and Canterbury had 16, approximately a third of the total of rugby union clubs. The new game also quickly began to make headway among New Zealand Maori.

But the outbreak of World War One meant that the hopes of the rugby league pioneers were not completely fulfilled. League recruited strongly in the industrial working-class areas of New Zealand, such as Auckland's docks and the West Coast's mines, but rugby union commanded the schools, the professions, and the majority of players. To be a 'leaguie' in New Zealand was (and is) to be an outsider, someone who was prepared to swim against the tide.

Tragically, Albert Baskerville, the man who brought the game to the country, did not live to see it played in his homeland. When the team arrived in Brisbane in May 1908, he complained of a chill, but still planned on playing in the upcoming game against Queensland. The day after the match he was diagnosed with influenza. Three days later it turned into pneumonia and he went into hospital. When his team-mates visited him late in the afternoon of Wednesday 20 May he had fallen into a coma. At six o'clock, surrounded by his team-mates, Albert Henry Baskerville died. He was just 25 years old.

In his short life, he had not only launched rugby league in New Zealand. On its way to Britain, his Professional All Blacks stopped over in Sydney and played three games against a professional Australian side. The Northern Union rule books did not arrive from England in time so the match was played under union rules. Nevertheless, the games were so successful that no-one could doubt rugby league had a future in Australia.

Rugby had been played in Sydney since 1865. Just as in Britain, it began as an elite pastime, but by the 1880s was becoming a mass spectator sport. As it began to spread across the industrial heartlands of New South Wales and Queensland, the entrance of working-class players into the game brought new problems for the leaders of Australian rugby union. They shared the RFU's fears that the influx of working-class players and spectators meant they would lose control of the game. In early 1898 the NSW Rugby Union investigated Billy Howe and George Outram for being paid to play in the previous season's matches against Queensland.

In 1904, 34,000 people saw the First Test between Australia and Britain at the Sydney Cricket Ground. Major club matches in the early 1900s could draw crowds of up to 20,000. Yet none of that cash found its way to players.

Rugby union's rigorous amateurism seemed unfair to the average Aussie. Tensions came to a head in 1907, when the rugby authorities closed the official medical insurance scheme for injured players. Despite 52,000 people paying over £2,500 to watch the All Blacks defeat NSW in July 1907, players were now forced to pay their own insurance premiums. A few weeks earlier one of rugby's star forwards, Alec Burdon, a docker, was unable to work after injuring his arm and shoulder in a match, but did not receive a penny in insurance. But at the same time, the Metropolitan Rugby Union, which ran the club game in Sydney, increased its secretary's salary to £250, about twice the annual average wage.

In secret, plans were already well underway for Northern Union rugby to begin in Sydney.

When the Auckland team visited in 1906, it appears George Smith discussed the possibility of starting a Northern Union rugby league competition. Victor Trumper, arguably Australia's greatest batsman before Don Bradman, and Labour Party politician Harry Hoyle were also meeting with discontented rugby players at Trumper's sports shop in Sydney's Market Street. As Baskerville was assembling his touring side in New Zealand, Glebe forward Peter Moir received a telegram from George Smith, who asked if Trumper's group would organise a team to play the New Zealanders in Sydney on their way to the UK. They agreed. The stage was set.

On 8 August 1907, 50 people – including eight club representatives and five first-grade team captains – assembled at Bateman's Crystal Hotel on Sydney's George Street and agreed to form the New South Wales Rugby Football League (NSWRFL). Its first task was to organise a committee to select a team to play the soon-to-be arriving Professional All Blacks. Four days later, Eastern Suburbs three-quarter Dally Messenger, the biggest name in Australian rugby, told the press he was joining the NSWRFL, one of 138 players who had signed up.

Shortly after, Baskerville's team arrived in Sydney. Dubbed the 'All Golds' by their opponents in the press, to emphasise their allegedly mercenary instincts, the rebels drew 20,000 people to the first of three matches against NSW on 17 August. A week later, Dally Messenger announced he would join Baskerville's tourists as a guest player.

The Northern Union had arrived down under.

In January 1908, rugby league clubs were established in the major districts of industrial Sydney. 'The league was formed because it was believed that the set of conditions controlling the [rugby] football unions were not suitable for the democracy and social conditions of the Australian people', future Labour MP Harry Hoyle told the founding meeting of the Glebe club. Nine clubs were admitted to the first NSWRFL premiership, which kicked off on 20 April 1908. The previous month in Brisbane, the Queensland Rugby Association had been founded and immediately affiliated with the NSWRFL.

Bolstered by the tremendous success of Baskerville's tour of Britain, the Northern Union agreed to an Australian tour the following season. In May, the inaugural rugby league Test match was played between Australia and New Zealand. For the first time, the Australians wore a Kangaroo on their jerseys. In October, the 'Kangaroos' began their first-ever tour of Britain. They struggled to adjust to the new game, winning only 17 of their 45 matches, and losing two and drawing one of the Tests. Blighted by an economic depression and terrible weather, the tour was a financial disaster, losing £418 and forcing tour manager James Giltinan into bankruptcy on his return home.

But ultimately, this did not matter. In 1910, the Northern Union organised the first British rugby league tour down under. It was captained by Salford's James Lomas who, in 1901, became the first player to command a £100 transfer fee when he moved across the Pennines from Bramley. Nicknamed the Lions, a full 40 years before the name was attached to rugby union's equivalent, the tourists cemented league's growing popularity as the leading football code in New South Wales and Queensland. These reciprocal visits established a deep rugby league bond, and the four-year cycle of tours to and from Australia became the fulcrum of the rugby league calendar. Most importantly, it now meant that rugby league was no longer just a northern game – it was now an international sport.

From Northern to National Union?

At the same time as the Northern Union was expanding into the southern hemisphere, it also seemed to be on the verge of breaking out of its northern heartland.

The issues that gave rise to the Northern Union were found wherever rugby was a mass spectator sport. Leicester, the biggest club in England after the 1895 split, was continually dogged by rumours it provided jobs and money to players. By 1907, the whispers of 'veiled professionalism' at the Tigers were so loud that the RFU was forced to investigate the club. If found guilty of professionalism, Leicester faced expulsion from rugby union.

The RFU's investigators found they used unaudited accounts, paid expenses without receipts and had offered one player cash not to leave the club. Despite this, they concluded that 'veiled professionalism did not now exist in the Rugby Union game'.

The controversy continued and another inquiry was ordered, yet when it reported back in January 1909 it also cleared Leicester of all charges. This was too much for RFU president Charles Crane, who resigned in protest at the whitewash. But the point of the inquiry was not to stop players being paid, but to ensure the RFU kept control of the game. Rugby union's leaders were quite prepared to suspend their amateur principles when it suited them. If Leicester had been expelled they would have joined the Northern Union, and the RFU's authority could have been fatally undermined. Unlike the hundreds of clubs in the north, Leicester were not seen as a threat to the RFU's control of rugby, so compromise was possible.

The last significant rebellions in English rugby union took place in Coventry and Devon, where rugby union still had significant working-class support. In late September 1909, the RFU opened an investigation into allegations that Coventry paid players. On 6 October, the club was suspended for three months, its secretary banned from the game, and five players suspended. The RFU even prevented the club's ground from being used until the new year. Coventry officials then met with the NU to discuss switching codes, with a significant faction of the club's members wanting to join immediately, while the rest waited to see if the RFU would reduce the ban.

Tired of being strung along by the Rugby Football Union, on 29 November the pro-NU group announced the creation of the Coventry NU football club. A week later, the RFU tried to outflank the new club by immediately lifting the ban on the old club. Faced with a revived union team and the rapidly growing popularity of Coventry City, Coventry NU struggled to compete in professional rugby league and eventually folded in 1913. Even so, the game left roots in the city and a Northern Union works league continued until after World War One.

In 1912, a similar series of events unfolded among rugby clubs in Devon and the South West. Faced with the burgeoning popularity of soccer clubs like Plymouth Argyle and Exeter City, a number of rugby clubs sought to revive the sport by joining the Northern Union and forming a Western

League. Eventually, clubs in Newton Abbot, Paignton, Plymouth, Teignmouth and Torquay enlisted in the NU.

In retaliation, on 30 November 1912, the RFU expelled or suspended 20 officials and players for professionalism. Among them was Jimmy Peters, the only black player to be selected for the England rugby union team until the 1980s. On Christmas Day 1912, he made his debut for the newly formed Plymouth Northern Union side against Coventry. But a lack of funds and organisational support meant that the clubs in the South West struggled to survive, and the RFU's strategically announced amnesty in April 1913 brought many rebels back into the union fold. By the end of the 1912-13 season, the uprising was over – and with it went the Northern Union's chance to become a national presence.

Yet the dream of national and international expansion would never disappear from rugby league.

5

•

Rugby at War

'[We were] a team which played rugby league football under rugby union rules.'
                                        – Harold Wagstaff, 1932.

In the Spring of 1916, Harold Wagstaff, Douglas Clark, Ben Gronow and Albert Rosenfeld were recruited to the Army Service Corps transport regiment based at Grove Park in South London. The First World War had begun on 4 August 1914, and when the 1914-15 rugby season ended the Northern Union suspended its league and cup competitions. Many clubs closed down for the duration of the war. But for Wagstaff and many other rugby league players, that did not mean that rugby had ended.

It was no coincidence that the Army Service Corps signed up these Huddersfield players, along with Oldham's Frank Holbrooke and Rochdale's Joe Corsi and Ernest Jones. Its commanding officer at Grove Park was Major R.V. Stanley, Oxford University's RFU representative. He assembled a team that dominated services' rugby union, winning 25 out of 26 games and scoring 1,110 points, while conceding just 41. In the process they broke the senior club record for points in a season. Their only loss was a narrow 6-3 to the United Services team that included eight rugby union internationals plus Wigan's Billy Seddon and Leeds' Willie Davies.

According to Harold Wagstaff, the secret of one of army rugby union's greatest sides was simple: they played rugby league under rugby union rules.

*****

Despite the rhetoric about national unity, rugby highlighted how social divisions in Britain remained as strong ever.

Even when playing in a match, Wagstaff had to address his Grove Park wing partner, the Harlequins' player lieutenant Nixon, as 'Sir'. Nixon simply referred to his centre as 'Wagstaff'. When the RFU temporarily lifted its ban on league players in the army and navy in October 1916, it explicitly excluded anyone working in factories. And at its first meeting after the Armistice, the RFU re-imposed its ban. Young men might be sent off to die in the same regiment, but they weren't allowed to play rugby in the same team.

World War One broke out a month before the 1914-15 season kicked off. On 8 September, the NU General Committee met and decided that matches should continue: '...as it is impossible for all men to take up active war service, and it is thought unwise to have no relaxation from the more serious objects of life ... [and that] all clubs be asked to encourage their players to join the army for active service, unless their employment is such that by not doing so they equally serve the country's welfare.'

The decision to continue playing did not stop players from enlisting. In September the St Helens' league suspended

44

activity after losing almost all of its players to the forces. The Bradford league was reduced to just four sides.

Swinton and Broughton Rangers both offered their grounds to the military and Wigan reserved one stand for free admission to men who had volunteered. Towards the end of the season, Joe Platt announced that 1,418 NU players – professional and amateur – had enlisted. But most players had good reasons for not immediately rushing to the colours. As *Athletic News* pointed out, unlike the usually single and often financially-independent young men of rugby union, many working-class players could 'not afford to throw their wives and families on the fickle charities of the public by enlisting'.

The new season was barely underway when it was gripped by another crisis. On 20 October, the NU imposed a 25 per cent wage cut on players. In response, players at Wigan, Halifax, Huddersfield, Rochdale and Oldham went on strike on Saturday 7 November, while Bradford and York players turned out under protest.

The following Friday, players' representatives from thirteen clubs met in Manchester and elected a four-man deputation to negotiate with NU officials. The four were major stars of the game: Harold Wagstaff, Gwyn Thomas, the 21-year-old full-back from Treherbert who had joined Wigan after captaining London Welsh, Wigan's Charlie Seeling, a tourist with the 1905 union and the 1907 league All Blacks, and Leeds's great Australian centre Dinny Campbell. Faced with a united front of players, the Northern Union rescinded the wage cuts.

Although the season continued, public interest waned as war casualties mounted and it became clear there would be no quick end to the conflict. Increasing numbers of spectators and players joined up. Gwyn Thomas enlisted in

December 1914 and, with Wigan's Lance Todd, became one of a handful of NU players to become a commissioned officer. The long working hours caused by war production in industrial areas also meant that fewer people had time to watch rugby. As soon as the season was over – in which Huddersfield won All Four Cups – the NU suspended operations until the end of the war.

Nevertheless, the professional game continued on a regional basis organised by the Lancashire and Yorkshire county committees. Despite the difficulties of war-time only four clubs didn't compete in the 1915-16 season, and Brighouse Rangers, Featherstone Rovers and St Helens Recreation were promoted to join the senior clubs, although Featherstone only lasted one season.

In 1916, Wakefield, Warrington and Widnes, who had closed for the 1915-16 season, recommenced playing. Barrow closed at the start of the war but soon re-established themselves and, boosted by an influx of players and spectators working on war production in the local shipyards, became one of the dominant teams of the war, winning the unofficial championship title in 1917-18. Dewsbury were even more successful, finishing champions in the 1915-16 and 1916-17 seasons, and attracting players and crowds due to the town's prominence as a manufacturer of woollen cloth for uniforms, and proximity to the Caulms Wood army base.

At the end of the 1914-15 season, the NU had also banned payments to players and allowed them to play for clubs based near their work or military base.

To no-one's surprise the payment ban was ignored and the relaxation of pre-war club registrations also created problems. In October 1917, Billy Batten was selected to play for both Dewsbury and Hull in the same match. He chose Dewsbury and helped them defeat his own team, 32-0.

Despite the supposed camaraderie of war-time, there is no evidence that the war led to more chivalrous behaviour. As the *Yorkshire Post* noted when six players were sent off in two Leeds matches in March 1917, games were 'fought in a much rougher and keener spirit than was the case in the normal competition days'. Nor were crowds better behaved. The Runcorn and Keighley grounds were shut after crowd trouble in March 1915, and the November 1917 derby between Broughton Rangers and Salford ended ten minutes early, after spectators joined in a fight between players.

In the armed forces, however, rugby league was almost never played. Officially it was not recognised as a sport and the army rugby authorities deferred to the RFU in all matters on and off the field.

In January 1915, a Miners' Battalion team of the King's Own Yorkshire Light Infantry played Featherstone Rovers at Otley rugby union ground to raise money for the widow of Corporal Dixon of Featherstone, but such matches were a very rare occurrence. Nor was rugby league played much at the front, although Rochdale winger and 1914 tourist Jack Robinson, who was badly wounded at Neuve Chappelle in March 1915, reported that they had played 'rugby' during the battle while bombs were dropping, saying that 'our boys out yonder will have their game of football under all sorts of conditions. It comes as a tonic and a relaxation from trench duty and I cannot understand anybody in England ever questioning the advisability of the game.'

Rugby union was the military sport and, according to the RFU's rules, rugby league players were banned from playing even when soldiers or sailors. But the skills and athleticism of NU players meant they were soon selected by forces' rugby union teams. In April 1916 a showpiece military match between the 'North of England' and an Australasian representative side was staged at Headingley. Featuring for the North were Harold Wagstaff, Ben Gronow and Douglas Clark of Huddersfield, plus Willie Davies, captain of Leeds. Oldham's Viv Farnsworth, Huddersfield's Tommy Gleeson, and Hull's Syd Deane and Jimmy Devereux were in the Australasian side. The NU players dominated, scoring fourteen points in the North's 13-11 win. Wagstaff, who had only ever seen one rugby union match previously, much less played in one, beat several opponents and ran half the field to score the try of the match.

But even rugby union played second fiddle to the most popular sport in the armed forces, soccer. Douglas Clark's war diary for 1917 records him playing in numerous soccer matches while in France, but only one game of 'rugby'. Harold Wagstaff also played soccer while stationed in Egypt, because no rugby of any kind was played. The danger of injury and the difficulty of playing on an improvised pitch naturally gave soccer an advantage. But it was also seen as a sport which all ranks could play to maintain morale. Rugby was generally viewed as a game almost exclusively for officers, soccer was the sport of the ranks, and the Northern Union game was squeezed out.

This did not stop rugby league players from attracting national attention. Just like the rugby league All-Stars of Harold Wagstaff's Grove Park army team, a similar side played for the Royal Navy depot at Devonport. This fielded nine NU players, captained by Leeds' Willie Davies and featuring at various times his team-mate and future international Joe Brittain, future Lions captain Jonty Parkin and Harold Buck, who became rugby league's first £1,000 transfer in 1921. Unlike the Grove Park side which broke up when its members were posted to France in April 1917, the Devonport side played together until the end of the war. They toured the North of England three times, playing against NU club sides and under NU rules.

But sport paled into insignificance when placed in the wider context of the slaughter that took place during the war. The Northern Union lost numerous players at all levels: Billy Jarman, Fred Longstaff and Walter Roman of the 1914 British tourists were killed, St Helens' 1907 New Zealand tourist Jum Turthill lost his life and Hull's Jack Harrison was posthumously awarded the Victoria Cross in 1917 for his bravery at Oppy Wood, in France.

At a club level, Leeds lost fifteen of 51 players who served, Widnes lost thirteen, Hull twelve and Swinton nine. But no total figures for NU players killed, either at professional or amateur level, were ever compiled. The only contemporary list was published by the *Athletic News* in 1919, which recorded that of the 760 professional players who served in the armed forces, 103 lost their lives.

We do not know how many amateur players were killed – only 42 clubs were listed in the Northern Union's 1919-20 *Official Guide*, down from 210 in the 1914-15 edition, but this was caused in large part by the economic and organisational difficulties facing clubs. Nor can we ever know how many thousands of rugby league supporters of NU clubs did not come back from the war to take their places back on the terraces.

Unlike rugby union, which glorified the deaths of its players, rugby league did not celebrate the war. The *Official Guide* for the first season afterwards did not even mention it. Wakefield Trinity's annual report for 1918-19 did not record that its captain Billy Beattie had been killed in action in France in 1917. The minute books of the Yorkshire Society of Referees contain not a single reference to the war at all between 1914 and 1918.

This was not due to indifference or lack of understanding. In the working-class communities of the industrial north the everyday experience of death and injury was profoundly different to that of the middle classes of rugby union. Even in peace time, death and serious injury at work was not unusual. Over 1,800 miners were killed in the coal industry in 1910, alongside 178,962 non-fatal injuries. In December that year, 344 men lost their lives in an explosion at the Pretoria pit in Westhoughton, near Wigan. Although even this could not compare with the 20,000 men slaughtered on the first day of the Battle of the Somme in 1916, it highlights the daily familiarity of working-class people with death and serious injury.

Nor was enthusiasm for the war as widespread as is often portrayed. Huddersfield was a centre of anti-war feeling. Peace meetings were staged regularly throughout the conflict and by 1917 the town had become, in the words of historian Cyril Pearce, 'a virtual citadel for the anti-war cause'. Throughout the summer of 1919, Britain was wracked by demonstrations of demobilised soldiers, often unemployed and angered by the way the government had treated them.

Glorification of the war by Northern Union officials and players was also rare. There was a suspicion that the game had been treated badly during war-time. The Army had given no support to the game and, in comparison to those of rugby union, the deaths of NU players had received little acknowledgement. When the war was mentioned it was generally at international matches. After the French rugby union had forced the cancellation of an exhibition match in Paris, SG Ball, manager of the 1920-21 Australian tourists, told his players that 'Northern Union players of England and Australia had helped France in the Great War, but had they been Germans the French Rugby Federation could not have treated them worse.'

The widespread hope that the war would lead to significant social change was expressed by a NU supporter during 1916 to *Athletic News*: 'As the war in this country is being fought on democratic lines, so will the future government of this land be on more democratic lines. There will be far less class distinction than we have been accustomed to. Merit will be recognised. Is it not possible that this may obtain in our sports?'

Yet at the end of the war Britain was as divided as it had ever been – and rugby no less so.

The social and geographic map of British sport in 1914 – and the relative strengths and weaknesses of league, union and soccer – were cemented in place by the war. After 1918, this map would not significantly change, and it presented a challenge with which rugby league would always grapple.

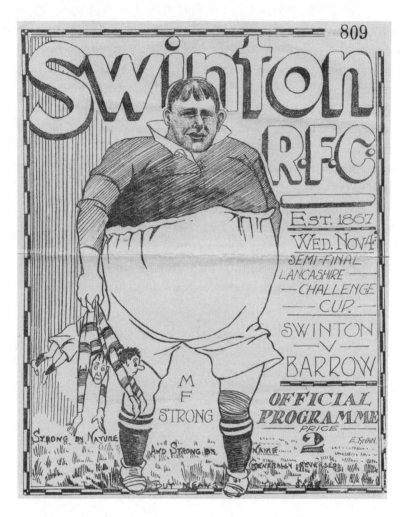

A Swinton programme cover from 1926

6

•

Hard Times in the Heartlands

'There is no loss of prestige in doing the most menial job [for your club], and men and women everywhere in the North are proud to help their club in this way.'
– Stanley Chadwick,
Rugby League Review editor, 1949.

Great teams should live on in the memory.

They perform unforgettable deeds and etch their names into the consciousness of the sport. Goldthorpe's 1908 Hunslet team, Wagstaff's 1914 Huddersfield side and Prescott's 1958 Lions echo down the ages. But occasionally, even some of the best sides get lost in the mists of time.

In 1925, Swinton finished at the top of the league for the first time ever. They narrowly lost the Championship final to the second-placed team, Hull KR, but they would go on to create one of the greatest sides in the history of the game. The following season they won the Challenge Cup for the first time in a generation, in 1927 they lifted the Championship for the first time and then, in 1928, they became only the third side to win the 'Grand Slam' of Championship. Challenge Cup, Lancashire Cup and Lancashire League. Captained by the wily centre Hector Halsall and marshalled by their Welsh stand-off Billo Rees and English-born Welsh scrum-half Bryn Evans, the Lions of Swinton swept all before them.

They won the Championship again in 1931 and 1935, and were Challenge Cup finalists in 1932, the only peacetime final not played at Wembley after 1929. They were a side of peerless players, boasting the titanic Martin Hodgson in the forwards, a man who hammered over goals like rivets into a ship's hull, including a gargantuan penalty goal of over 77 yards in 1940.

Yet the deeds of this amazing side have been all but forgotten. The club never appeared at Wembley and, after 1935, didn't contest a Challenge Cup or Championship final, although they did finish top of the first division in 1963 and 1964. When Manchester rugby league in the inter-war years is remembered, it is the Lions' deadliest rivals, Gus Risman's Salford, who are recalled. Swinton's fate is testimony to the fickleness of the sporting memory, but it is also an example of the deep economic difficulties that rugby league clubs faced in the 1930s.

In 1929, at the peak of their powers, Swinton moved into a brand new ground at Station Road. On March 22 that year, 22,000 crammed into the stadium to see it opened with a 9-3 victory over Wigan. The future could not be brighter. But almost exactly six months later, on October 24, Wall Street crashed and the world plunged into the Great Depression.

Swinton would never fully recover from it, and were to become the great forgotten team.

*****

When World War One ended, the game found itself riding on the crest of a popularity boom. By 1922, the finals of all four major tournaments had recorded their highest ever attendances, while Dewsbury, Hull KR and Rochdale Hornets set crowd records which still stand today.

Symbolising the game's new riches, Leeds purchased Hunslet's star three-quarter Harold Buck in 1921 for £1,000, the first player to be transferred for a four figure sum. Many clubs invested heavily in their stadia. Hull spent almost £2,000 on their Boulevard ground, Halifax bought Thrum Hall for £8,000 and Hull KR's brand new Craven Park opened in 1922 at a cost of more than £18,000.

The boom did not last. From late 1921, coal and textiles, the industrial foundations upon which northern rugby was built, fell into economic depression. Cotton exports, life-force of towns like Oldham, Rochdale and to a lesser extent Wigan, hit half their 1913 levels. Exports of wool from West Yorkshire collapsed. Coal, the black thread that ran through the heart of the game, saw exports shrink to a third of their pre-war level. Unemployment leapt to two million in June 1922 and by 1923 wages had dropped to 40 per cent less than in 1914.

Almost every rugby league club struggled. Bradford, York and Rochdale were put under the RFL's financial control between 1927 and 1930. Barrow, Swinton and Featherstone Rovers needed major loans from the RFL to stay alive. Each town suffered the effects of the depression. Bradford saw the the decline of the wool trade, Barrow by the halving of the shipbuilding workforce during the 1920s, Rochdale due to the contraction of the cotton trade, while Leigh, Swinton and Featherstone were bludgeoned by coal's collapse.

Falling wage levels and rising unemployment meant that clubs often found that their crowds fell regardless of on-field success. Hull's average attendance halved from 12,692 in 1921 to 6,212 in 1926, despite finishing in the top four in both seasons. Featherstone averaged 3,470 spectators in their first professional season in 1920-21, but never matched it again before 1940. In March 1930, just 200 supporters watched them play Bradford and in the 1933-34 season crowds at Post Office Road averaged less than 1,000.

Although accurate crowd figures for league matches were not recorded by the RFL until the late 1940s, cup and league crowds appear to recover from the mid-1930s. Both Leeds and Bradford averaged over 12,000 spectators per league match in 1938-39. Barrow's average gate rose from 6,720 in 1931-32 to 9,092 in 1938-39, as they became one of the leading clubs in the league. Record attendances were established for the Challenge Cup and Yorkshire Cup finals, while new records of over 60,000 were seen both for a Challenge Cup semi-final and the Championship final. Average attendances for Challenge Cup matches before Wembley also rose from 11,583 in 1934 to 15,296 in 1939, while at Castleford, Hull and Salford new crowd records were set in this period.

As league struggled, soccer extended its popularity and its crowds dwarfed those of every other sport. Manchester City won the FA Cup in 1934 and attracted over 493,000 people to their cup matches, 58,000 more than those who watched all of that year's Challenge Cup games. The threat of the round-ball game was never far from the minds of rugby league administrators. Wigan Borough, Halifax Town, Castleford Town and Wakefield City applied to join the Football League in 1921, with the first two being successful. Halifax Town struggled and Wigan Borough resigned from the Football League in 1931, owing almost £30,000. It had become harder for soccer to dislodge rugby in the smaller northern towns than it was in big cities, not least because the costs of paying full-time professional players were so much higher. Even so, in 1932 Salford manager Lance Todd called for summer rugby, partly to avoid bad weather – more than a hundred games were cancelled in the 1931-32 season – but also to avoid competing with soccer.

The fall in rugby league attendances meant clubs which invested heavily in their stadia in the 1920s faced almost intractable problems. Despite initial success, Hull KR were forced to sell their Craven Park ground in 1938 to a greyhound company for a loss of over £6,500. Swinton faced similar issues after buying their Station Road ground in 1929. Declining crowds and on-field failure meant that mortgage repayments took an increasing portion of the club's declining income. They were caught in a vicious circle with less to spend on players, meaning a weaker team that did not attract new spectators caused revenue to fall even further. But this was not always appreciated by Swinton supporters: 'What's the point of having a good shop if there's nothing to show in window?' complained one fan, at the club's 1934 general meeting, about the money spent on the stadium.

Nationwide unemployment during the inter-war years averaged fourteen per cent, but it was much higher in rugby league's heartlands. In 1921, Warrington had donated 350 season tickets to their local Unemployed Committee, but at the end of the year the RFL dismissed calls to allow the unemployed into matches for free by stating '...no such admission of unemployed to matches be granted or allowed by any of its clubs'. Even so, in September 1922 Barrow defied the RFL's official minimum admission of one shilling and reduced their cheapest ticket to ninepence, much to the annoyance of the local soccer club which begged the Football League to be allowed to do the same.

The clamour for the RFL to reduce admission charges

grew throughout the 1920s, especially when pit-owners locked out miners from April to November 1926.

In August 1926, the *St Helens Newspaper & Advertiser* asked the RFL to consider the thousands 'who will have to stand outside gates and listen to the cheers of the favoured ones within. They have not the money to pay even the modest admission fee charged.'

In September, unemployed Leigh supporters, many of them miners, broke through the gates of the club's Mather Lane ground to see their side play the New Zealand tourists. Many clubs simply ignored the RFL during the miners' lock-out and allowed them in for sixpence. This was still beyond many fans, but what the pocket lacked was made up for by the ingenuity of supporters, as a reporter described at a match at Featherstone:

> Yard walls and bedroom windows were used as grandstands, or rather grand sit-downs, for I noticed over a hundred lads perched rather precariously on one wall. They simply didn't get excited or they would have clattered down into the passage. Some of the old colliery houses had trap-doors on the roof and from each tiny trap-door there peeped forth a pair of eyes intently watching the game. It was for all the world like one of Heath Robinson's sketches.

Clubs also usually allowed unemployed fans in at reduced prices after half-time. Alf Ellaby, the great St Helens winger, later recalled how the roar of the home crowd became much louder in the second half of matches because of the number of unemployed spectators allowed in during the interval.

Finally, in December 1932, the RFL voted to allow the

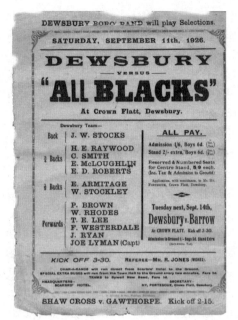

DEWSBURY BORO' BAND will play Selections.

SATURDAY, SEPTEMBER 11th, 1926.

DEWSBURY

— VERSUS —

"ALL BLACKS"

At Crown Flatt, Dewsbury.

Dewsbury Team—

		ALL PAY.
Back	J. W. STOCKS	
¾ Backs	H. E. RAYWOOD C. SMITH E. McLOUGHLIN E. D. ROBERTS	Admission 1/6, Boys 6d. Stand 2/- extra, Boys 6d. Reserved & Numbered Seats for Centre Stand, 5/- each. (Inc. Tax & Admission to Ground)
½ Backs	E. ARMITAGE W. STOCKLEY	Application, with remittance, to Mr. Hy. Fortescue, Crown Flatt, Dewsbury.
Forwards	P. BROWN W. RHODES T. E. LEE F. WESTERDALE J. RYAN JOE LYMAN (Capt)	Tuesday next, Sept. 14th, **Dewsbury v. Barrow** At CROWN FLATT. Kick off 3-30. Admission to Ground 1/- Boys 6d. Stand Extra

KICK OFF 3-30.   REFEREE—MR. R. JONES (WIGAN).

CHAR-A-BANCS will run direct from Scarbro' Hotel to the Ground. SPECIAL EXTRA BUSES will run from the Town Hall to the Ground every two minutes, Fare 2d. TRAMS to Bywell New Road, Fare 1d. HEADQUARTERS— SCARBRO' HOTEL. SECRETARY— HY. FORTESCUE, Crown Flatt, Dewsbury.

SHAW CROSS v. GAWTHORPE. Kick off 2-15.

Dewsbury versus New Zealand poster from September 1926

unemployed into league, but not cup, matches for sixpence, a privilege also extended to 'ladies'. This was initially very successful. At the 1936 Cumberland versus Yorkshire game at Workington, the press estimated that half of the 10,600 crowd were unemployed. In 1930, a Featherstone versus Castleford derby saw 1,800 of the record 9,334 fans admitted at the sixpenny unemployed rate.

Despite the economic hardship of the interwar years, spectator disorder was rare. There were just 19 incidents of crowd misbehaviour reported to the RFL, compared to 30 between 1895 and 1910. At the 1922 Challenge Cup final at Headingley a thousand Rochdale fans arrived late and threatened to break down the gates, until officials let them all in for free. Apart from two instances of stone-throwing at visiting players and a fracas at Bradford between home supporters and Dewsbury players in April 1926, every other incident was directed at match officials. The most serious took place in 1937, when a touch judge was knocked out by a stone thrown from the crowd at Hull KR. Anxious to avoid their ground being closed, the club claimed that the official had actually fainted! The RFL didn't believe them and closed Craven Park for a fortnight.

However, during these two decades of severe economic depression in the North of England, only one professional club in the rugby league heartland disappeared.

That side was St Helens Recreation, essentially the works' side of local glassmakers Pilkington, who closed down the team at the end of the 1938-39 season. Pilkingtons had underwritten eighteen consecutive loss-making seasons but had never been completely comfortable with rugby league. Despite a respectable playing record (which included winning the Lancashire League and the Lancashire Cup), 'Recs', as they were known, were competing for crowds with St Helens in a town hit especially hard by the problems of the coal industry. Unlike Wigan Highfield, who had joined the League in 1922, moved to London in 1933 and then on to Liverpool in 1934, Pilkington's ownership of the club meant it could not try to improve its finances by moving to a different town.

Other clubs facing financial difficulties tried to raise additional capital by becoming a limited company and issuing shares. But this was not necessarily a route to economic health. Bramley only sold 700 of their 2,000 shares when they became a company in 1927. Ten years later, St Helens sold fewer than 6,000 of their 8,000 issued shares. Keighley and Rochdale had similar problems and only Halifax's 1936 conversion was successful. At the end of the 1930s, Leigh and Rochdale reverted back to being members' clubs.

The other popular approach was to acquire the patronage of local businessmen.

In 1931, Keighley were saved from closure by two local businessmen. Featherstone's new stand and terracing was paid for by Abraham Bullock, owner of a local bus company. York were heavily reliant on Sir William Forster-Todd until the late 1920s. Local brewers Greenall Whitley underwrote St Helens' purchase of the Knowsley Road ground in 1925. In 1931, Barrow named their new stadium Craven Park after C.W. Craven, the managing director of the local Armstrong-Vickers naval shipyard. When Wigan met Welsh international rugby union winger and policeman Arthur Bassett in the late 1930s, the Chief Constable of Wigan went along to offer him a job if he joined the club.

Some clubs tried to increase income by diversifying, usually into speedway or greyhound racing, the new two 'boom' sports of the late 1920s. Barrow, Rochdale and both Hull clubs experimented with these in the early 1930s. One reason for Hull KR's survival in the 1930s seems to be due to the income it received from greyhound racing at its Craven Park stadium. Rovers also staged baseball during the summer months, as did other clubs in the late 1930s. In 1936, Bradford raised over £500 by renting out Odsal for baseball matches. But not all clubs were successful. Rochdale ended speedway after two years, citing poor crowds.

Diversification, but of a unique kind, was a major reason for the success of Leeds rugby league club.

The club owned Headingley stadium, its joint-home with Yorkshire County Cricket Club during the county's golden age and a major Test match cricket venue. In 1927, Leeds announced its first-ever dividend payment to shareholders. The financial importance of cricket to Leeds is illustrated by their profit of £4,093 in the 1930-31 season, which exceeded the total profits of every other league club combined. In contrast, Swinton, who defeated them, 14-7, in that season's Championship final, recorded a loss of £76 in the same season.

But for most clubs the key factor in their survival was the activities of their supporters. Supporters' clubs were first formed after the First World War and by 1923 there were enough in Yorkshire to start a county federation.

In its first season, the federation reported that Featherstone supporters raised £100 to assist the purchase of the Post Office Road ground and Huddersfield supporters raised £114 to pay the club's heating bills. Bramley, Castleford, Hunslet, Keighley and Wakefield fans also raised money for ground improvements. Supporters' clubs might organise player testimonial funds. Huddersfield's fans collected almost £200 for Ben Gronow, and Bramley's Lou Marshall was presented with £104 from their activities.

In 1929, Bradford's supporters took over the running of the club's reserve team. In the mid-1920s Leigh supporters raised money with an annual brass band contest. In 1938, St Helens' fans raised £250 of the £275 transfer fee that brought Liverpool Stanley forward George Davies to the club. By 1946, Huddersfield supporters' club had collected around £4,800 since it began in 1921.

As well as fund-raising, many supporters' clubs provided other services, all of it unpaid. At Bramley, Keighley and Wakefield, they produced the match-day programmes. Most, if not all, organised excursions to away matches and to London for the Challenge Cup final. Many also provided refreshment facilities for spectators.

Batley, Bradford, Hunslet and York organised end of season workshops competitions, factory team tournaments held at the club's ground. They brought both gate takings and potential new players to the club. In 1925, the Yorkshire Federation organised the county's inter-town rugby league for boys aged between 14 and 16-years-old. The spirit of self-sacrifice and collectivity that underpinned this work was articulated by the journalist and staunch Huddersfield fan Stanley Chadwick:

> Members of Northern League clubs are not only content to attend home matches but organise motor coach trips to away matches; run whist drives and concerts to augment club funds; scrub the pavilion floor, serve in the dry canteen, assist with programme selling, encourage the junior leagues, and indulge in many other activities. There is no loss of prestige in doing the most menial job, and men and women everywhere in the North are proud to help their club in this way.

Club directors were not always supportive. Those of Keighley, Swinton and York refused to recognise their supporters' clubs following criticism of their teams by the fans. But, on the whole, provided they did not publicly deride club management or the RFL, supporters' clubs were highly valued by officials. RFL secretary John Wilson regularly met the Yorkshire Federation, and in 1928 the RFL insisted that two supporters' representatives should sit on the reconstituted York club committee. Halifax and Huddersfield supporters' clubs also had a seat on their club management committees.

Especially in times of crisis, clubs relied on support from wider sections of their local communities too.

In 1926, Featherstone miners'welfare club bought the club's Post Office Road ground from its owners and rented it back to them. In June 1934 over 1,000 miners at the town's two pits voted for a weekly deduction of three pence to be taken from their wages and given to the club.

In the early 1930s, Keighley organised a successful 'Shilling Fund', where local people were asked to give a shilling to club funds.

To help furnish the new Odsal stadium in 1934, Bradford offered ownership of a strip of the pitch's turf for sixpence. The club calculated that the pitch comprised 49,500 such strips and hoped to raise over £1,230. In the end, it was more than pleased with the £900 the scheme delivered.

In the final analysis, it was volunteer and community support which ensured rugby league's survival during the Great Depression.

Professional sport has always been a pyramid which relies on the patronage of the rich at the top, but for its daily survival it depends on the community of thousands of enthusiasts and volunteers. When patronage was not available, it was supporters of all types – from the die-hard to the fair-weather – whose efforts and resources ensured the survival of their rugby league club.

7
·
Rebel Players in the Rebel Sport

*'Stocky men with short upper lips and jutting long
chins, men who roll a little in their walk and carry
their heads stiffly, twelve stone of combative instinct.'*
— J.B. Priestley, *Apes and Angels, 1928.*

Jonty Parkin was the archetype of the rugby league scrum-
half. Tough, smart, cocky and argumentative, he viewed the
referee as just as much of an opponent as the opposing team.

Born in 1894, into a mining family in the village of
Sharlston (like fellow Hall of Fame member, Neil Fox), Parkin
made his debut for Wakefield Trinity as a teenager in 1913.
As soon as World War One was over he was picked for the
1920 Lions' trip to Australia and New Zealand, the first of his
three tours. The following season, he captained the national
side for the first time, led the 1924 and 1928 Lions and
skippered the team for a decade.

Jonty rose to the top despite Wakefield's indifferent
form in the 1920s. His leadership skills were matched only
by his predecessor as Lions' captain, Harold Wagstaff, but

unlike Wagstaff, Parkin also sought to exploit the weaknesses of those in authority. Fans often claimed he was refereeing matches. In the 1924 Yorkshire Cup semi-final, a Trinity kick rolled over the dead-ball line and Leeds's full-back, Syd Walmsley, threw it forward to his captain on the 25-yard line. Seeing the referee lagging behind the play, Parkin turned to him and claimed it was a forward pass. Unsighted, the referee blew the whistle for a scrum – and Parkin fed the ball, picked it up and scored under the posts for a Trinity win.

In his attitude to officials on and off the field, Jonty Parkin created the template that all other rugby league players followed.

*****

Although the game was often inaccurately called the professional code of rugby, there were very few full-time professional rugby league players until the 1980s.

Of the 26 who went on the 1928 Lions' tour to Australia and New Zealand, only four gave their occupation as 'footballer'. Throughout the inter-war years, virtually every player had a full-time job outside of the game, not least because their rugby earnings were rarely enough to live on. For example, in the 1920-21 season Halifax players received £4 for a win and £2/10 shillings for a loss. In 1934, the club paid £4/10 shillings for a home win and £5 for an away win. But Halifax were an exception. Few other clubs could afford such high wage levels.

In 1938, St Helens were paying £2/10 shillings for a home win, £3/5 shillings for a win in Yorkshire, but only £1/10 shillings for a loss. Dai Davies signed for Broughton Rangers in 1926 for £3 per win and £1/10 shillings for a loss. Further down the scale, Featherstone paid just £1/10 shillings per win in the 1920s. During the 1936-37 season, Leigh players' wages were slashed to just £1 per match win, lose or draw. This was low pay compared to soccer players – in 1922 the Football League had set the maximum weekly wage at £8 plus £2 per match win bonus, rarely matched in rugby.

Star players were generally paid more than their less high-profile team-mates. Jonty Parkin demanded and was given a fixed £10 per game when he moved to Hull KR in 1930. For a match against Wigan in March 1932, St Helens star winger Alf Ellaby received £9, four pounds more than anyone else. In the 1929-30 season his losing pay was £7 per match, more than the winning pay of the rest of the side. Despite this, his match-winning talent was such that few, if any, team-mates complained.

Welsh rugby union converts were also often paid higher wages than their northern team-mates.

George Lewis moved to St Helens from Pontypool in 1922, paid £5/10 shillings for a win, £4 a draw and £3 loss. Players selected to tour Australia and New Zealand also gained financially. One-third of the tour profits were divided between the players, leading to bonuses of between £100 and £200 which in some cases could equal the annual wage from a player's non-rugby job.

Players also sometimes received perks from local businessmen. Towards the end of the 1915 Championship final, Harold Wagstaff sliced through the Leeds defence and was surprised to find forward Fred Longstaff burst through in support shouting 'suit, suit, suit'. A few days earlier, a local tailor had promised Wagstaff a new suit if he scored a try. Longstaff complained to the tailor that the backs always got the gifts, so the tailor told Longstaff he could also have a suit if he scored a try.

Rugby league wages were rarely enough to live on, but

were a useful supplement to a players' weekly wage from his full-time job outside the game.

Miners' average weekly wages were just over £2/7 shillings in 1935, and a male textile worker took home an average of £2/16 shillings in 1938. Even skilled workers averaged only £3 and 15 shillings in 1936. The addition of an extra two or three pounds a week from rugby made a considerable difference to the living standards enjoyed by a working-class family. And the fact that players drew their primary income from outside of rugby was an important factor in sustaining the sport economically. Unlike top soccer sides, no club could afford to pay players when they were not playing, either through injury or in the off-season.

One advantage that league did have over soccer was that the RFL did not put a ceiling on signing-on fees, so players who were courted by soccer and rugby league clubs, such as England rugby union full-back Jim Brough or the young Gus Risman, often opted for league over soccer.

Jim Brough explained in 1948 why he rejected Liverpool FC:

> What signing-on fee would I receive? When told the maximum allowed by the FA was only £10, I immediately lost interest, for it compared very unfavourably with Swinton's recent offer of £350. Of course, there was a guaranteed benefit of £650 every five years, but that seemed a long way off when I could get this amount from a Rugby League club at once.

The difference a large signing-on fee could make to player was explained by Salford manager Lance Todd in 1939:

The money has been paid over into a bank and a banking account opened with the amount paid, so that the player starts with that great and glorious feeling of 'having money in the bank' ... with application to his work and his football, the player's opportunity of getting away from what in many cases might mean a lifetime's grind, is great.

Signing-on fees were also psychologically very persuasive. When a club official visited the home of a player, opened his briefcase, and placed a large amount of cash in front of its intended recipient, few could resist.

The signing-on fee was also one of the biggest financial incentives for Welsh union players to switch, not least because it was tax-free, a loophole justified by Master of the Rolls, Lord Denning, who ruled in a 1964 court case that losing one's amateur status was so terrible that only monetary compensation could make up for it. Nevertheless, the highest signing-on fees during this period probably went to Australian rugby league stars. Dave Brown received £1,000 for signing for Warrington from Eastern Suburbs in 1936. Vic Hey left Parramatta for Leeds for £1,400, an amount higher than the record transfer fee at that time.

As well as the signing-on fee, high-profile captures were provided with jobs, often thanks to links with local companies.

Greenall Whitley brewery in St Helens frequently helped the club's players become public house landlords. Huddersfield's connections with the local textiles industry provided office or sales jobs to Fartown stars. For many Welsh rugby-playing miners who went north, not having to work underground was a strong factor in switching to league.

For some, the jobs offered the possibility of a small elevation in social status. Within six years of signing for Huddersfield in 1933, Australian Ray Markham was appointed assistant superintendent of Huddersfield Corporation's markets and fairs department.

Those fortunate to play the game for ten years with the same club could also benefit from a testimonial season. For the best-loved, this could raise significant sums. In 1920, Billy Batten received £1,079 from grateful Hull supporters. Even the £200 raised for Huddersfield forward Henry Tiffany, in 1936, was enough for him to buy a house. However, very few players actually had a career of ten years in the game, let alone with a single club. A survey of Wigan players'careers in the inter-war years shows that fewer than six per cent played for a decade or more, while 54 per cent lasted two seasons or less.

The general attitude of club directors towards players was demonstrated by Broughton Rangers' and RFL chairman Fred Kennedy. When Welsh half-back Dai Davies asked for a transfer Kennedy refused, telling him: 'We made you. Don't you forget that'. However, Davies's hatred of authority was at least the equal of his talent and he eventually negotiated his own transfer to Warrington. When a financial crisis forced St Helens to put Alf Ellaby on the transfer list, Ellaby discovered that he had been sold to Broughton Rangers without being told:

> The Broughton Rangers secretary arrived and said, 'We've signed you from St Helens.' I replied, 'Haven't you considered me?' He had a paint business and I said, 'You're not buying a gallon of paint! I'm not going to play for you. I couldn't play well in your team.'

Alf Ellaby kicked up a fuss when sold to Broughton Rangers

His obstinacy paid off and he eventually moved to Wigan, the club of his choice.

The attitude of most players to officials was reflected by Vic Hey who wrote that 'many club directors are not very well versed in rugby league football ... they think that a footballer is a machine.' This type of belief was behind the formation of the Northern Rugby Union Players' Union (NRUPU) in November 1920. The idea of a players' union had been suggested as early as 1909 and re-emerged among the 1920 tourists to Australia and New Zealand tourists. On their return home the NRUPU was founded in Huddersfield with Harold Wagstaff as its chair and Huddersfield's star Welsh full-back Gwyn Thomas as secretary/treasurer. Such major names, coupled with increasing discontent among players – in January 1919 Oldham players went on strike for higher match fees, and Salford and Barrow players struck over payments in 1920 – ensured the union had to be taken seriously.

The union's goals were to promote friendship among players, redress grievances, modify the transfer system to the advantage of the players and guarantee players a benefit after six years continuous service with one club. Despite the moderation of these demands, the NU was unwilling to compromise in any significant way and much of 1921 was spent skirmishing over the NU's refusal to recognise the NRUPU.

In August 1922, the union announced it would strike at the start of the season if the NU still refused to negotiate. Players also threatened to strike at Barrow, Halifax and Hull over match fees. Under pressure, the NU agreed to meet if the strike threat was withdrawn, and the two sides did on 27 September. Deadlock resulted, but just a few weeks later Gwyn Thomas, its driving force, fled to America because of what in later years he called his 'irresponsibility' involving a woman. The union quickly disintegrated having been out-manoeuvred by NU officials, and it was formally dissolved in May 1923.

After the collapse of the union, only Bramley, in March 1926, and Leigh, in February 1931, were hit by players' strikes during the interwar years. Unlike in industry, it was easy for NU clubs to 'divide and rule' by secretly paying selected players to undermine collective action. This was seen in the Leigh strike, when players protested about a pay cut by refusing to play a match against Bradford. Leigh's directors enlisted the reserve team to strike break and play instead, and the reserves promptly defeated Bradford, 8-0!

One of the difficulties in organising a players' union was the fact most had full-time jobs outside of the sport and were not dependent on their rugby earnings. On the other hand, working in a factory or pit meant league players probably had more political consciousness than their soccer counterparts.

In 1930, the Communist Party claimed 'at least one international' was a party member in the Wigan area and that other players were sympathetic to it. Dai Davies, a Welshman who went north to play for Batley, and Joe Latus, a prominent Hull FC supporter and perennial candidate for the club's board of directors, fought with the International Brigades in the Spanish Civil War.

At least one other, Bramley and Bradford player John Clynes, was rumoured to have fought against Franco. Davies also claimed that radical politics prevented him and another Welshman, Broughton's Evan Phillips, from ever being selected for the Welsh rugby union side.

This left-wing political tradition continued after the Second World War, most notably by Stan Chadwick, who combined the editorship of *Rugby League Review* with membership of the Independent Labour Party, and Norman Berry, a Communist Party member who edited the *Rugby League Gazette*.

This connection between rugby league and politics is reflected in the story of how Wigan became known as the 'pie-eaters'. Its origins lay not in the town's love of meat pies, but from 1926 and the mine-owners' seven-months' lock-out of miners. Miners in Wigan were accused, particularly by those in St Helens, of returning to work early and being forced to eat humble pie by the mine owners. By the second week of October 1926, miners at five Wigan pits voted to return to work (some in the Leigh coalfield had returned as early as September 28). But in St Helens, only 90 men out of 10,000 returned to work before the union was finally forced to admit defeat in November. As Charles Forman recorded in *Industrial Town*, his oral history of St Helens, this refusal to submit was still a source of pride 50 years later. 'Nowhere was more solid than St Helens,' one old miner told him. 'It was organised here to the last moment.' A year later, the small town of St Helens could boast two professional rugby league teams and eight branches of the Communist Party.

The demise of the players' union left players with no collective means of redress against their employers. Walking out on a club would in all likelihood spell the end of their careers. Few players had either the means or the self-confidence to emulate Jonty Parkin.

In 1930, Wakefield reduced their players' wages but Parkin objected and was put on the transfer list at £100. He paid the fee himself and negotiated with other clubs, demanding a £300 signing-on fee and £8 per match, and eventually joined Hull KR. No-one would ever buy themselves again because the RFL promptly outlawed players paying their own transfer fees. But Jonty Parkin's hostility to authority was a characteristic shared wherever players picked up a rugby league ball or supporters watched them do so.

8
•

Up for the Cup down South

*'The playing of our Cup Final in London has never
been looked upon as propaganda in the usual sense of
the term but rather to give our game a standing of
national importance.'*
– Tom Ashcroft, St Helens Recs chairman, 1934.

It was a bit of a struggle, for two middle-aged men to climb
the dozens of narrow steps to the top of the twin towers of
Wembley stadium.

One of them was John Wilson, who had been appointed
RFL secretary in 1920. A Scotsman, he was involved with Hull
Kingston Rovers before World War One, but had made his
name as a cyclist and rode in the 1912 Olympic Games in
Stockholm. His companion on the journey to the top of
Wembley was Fred Kennedy, a builders' merchant from
Manchester who was chairman of Broughton Rangers and,
for the 1928-29 season, the RFL.

When they finally hauled themselves, sweating and
breathless, to the top of the steps, both men realised it had

been worth it. They looked out over the vast expanse of grass and terraces, and marvelled at the sheer magnificence of the arena. They agreed there and then that this was the only place Rugby League's showcase fixture should be played. They returned North and, a week later, the RFL Council made the historic decision that the Challenge Cup final would, in 1929, be played at Wembley.

It was the culmination of a debate begun by the Reverend Frank Chambers, then retired but still the game's most famous referee, who had proposed moving the Cup final to London at a 1928 meeting of the Yorkshire Society of Referees. He'd pointed to the tremendous excitement in his home town, caused by Huddersfield Town's impending visit to Wembley for the 1928 FA Cup final, the first by a soccer side in a rugby league area. Later that year, the RFL's annual general meeting agreed in principle to move its own final to the English capital.

A new era had begun for rugby league.

*****

The RFL opened negotiations with Wembley and Crystal Palace, the two biggest stadia in London and, on 17 October 1928, Wilson and Kennedy made their visit to inspect both grounds.

Wembley was always the clear favourite.

The success of the FA Cup final since it moved there in 1923 was something the RFL wanted to emulate. But it was also attracted by the prestige of the Empire Stadium, as Wembley was officially known.

As Bolton Wanderers, Newcastle United, Sheffield United and Blackburn Rovers had shown by winning the FA Cup at its new home, Wembley was an arena in which northern towns and cities could gain prominence on the national stage.

Originally built for the 1924 British Empire Exhibition, the stadium was the pet project of the Prince of Wales, the future Edward VIII, who told the 1921 Imperial Conference of Dominions' prime ministers that the exhibition would house a 'great national sports ground' which the FA was considering for the home of the Cup final. The exhibition itself lost around £10 million and the stadium became a white elephant. However, its image changed dramatically with the first soccer match held there: the 1923 'White Horse' FA Cup final when 200,000 people crammed into the stadium and were seemingly controlled by a single policeman on a white horse.

As the first Wembley final approached, the RFL was determined 'to make it an annual event in the sporting calendar'. It wrote to all clubs to encourage them to form savings clubs to help supporters regularly deposit funds to go to London. Posters and leaflets were produced for clubs to distribute and speakers arranged for public meetings. In the south, adverts were placed in local newspapers and 15,000 leaflets cheekily distributed at England's rugby union matches against Wales and Ireland at Twickenham. The minimum admission cost was set at a bargain two shillings, while the best seats were priced at ten shillings and sixpence. All matches were cancelled on Cup final day so that everyone was free to make the historic journey south.

This was a return to pre-1895 northern rugby traditions, when savings clubs were set up by supporters to save for trips to the Yorkshire Cup final or club tours to London or South Wales at Christmas and Easter.

In 1929, a trip to London was still a rarity for most northerners, and didn't fail to generate a sense of excitement.

Around 20,000 people travelled south to see Dewsbury play Wigan in a Challenge Cup final which symbolised the state of the sport in 1929. The cosmopolitan all-stars of Wigan included five Welshmen, two New Zealanders, a Scot and just three Lancastrians. Their opponents Dewsbury had just one player not born in Yorkshire. Wigan won by 13 points to 2, and despite not being a memorable game, the first Wembley final drew a crowd of 41,500 and was universally acclaimed a success.

The journey to Wembley quickly became seen as a pilgrimage. The Hull playwright Alan Plater even wrote a 1975 TV series, *Trinity Tales*, based on Chaucer's *Canterbury Tales*, which followed a group of supporters on their Cup final trip. Trains and buses, or charabancs in the 1930s, left the two competing towns long before dawn on the Saturday morning, bursting with supporters decked out in their team's colours. But this was not just about the finalists.

The Cup final became a festival of rugby league, and the tradition was soon established that all towns and villages in rugby league areas organised trips down south. In towns where clubs reached the final, employers often allowed workers time off work to go to Wembley. Pratt's Engineering in Halifax not only gave their workers the Saturday off to go to the 1939 Cup final, but also paid the fares for 200 of them, thus helping to swell the ranks of Halifax supporters to 8,000.

In 1934, another tradition commenced when 1,500 schoolchildren made the trip south to watch Hunslet face Widnes, thanks to the RFL's decision to allow pupils into the match for free. By the end of the decade over 5,000 were going to Wembley and, despite the subsequent withdrawal of free entry, school trips from across the north became a permanent feature of the Cup final experience (and also gave the author his first trip to London in 1975).

The chance to see London became one of the biggest selling points for Cup final excursions in the 1930s and 1940s. 'Do you want to see the sights of London? Do you want to see the Rugby League Cup final? Do you want the trip of a lifetime?' asked a leaflet issued by Wakefield Trinity to advertise their chartered train to Wembley in 1938.

The fact that the final was not always sold out meant that, unlike the FA Cup final, there was ample opportunity for families to make the trip and for supporters to visit Wembley every year, regardless of which teams were playing, adding to its carnival-like atmosphere. When they arrived in the capital, supporters usually disembarked in central London and went sightseeing before the match. One Huddersfield supporter described his trip to see the 1933 final:

> Upon arrival in London the parties split up into their various groups and hurried off in diverse directions, as the fancy took them, each anxious to see the part of London they planned to see, and very quickly the 'Claret and Gold' [Huddersfield colours] was to be seen all over the City ... [I went on] a stroll through the streets of the City to the 'hub of the universe', Piccadilly, meeting from time to time groups of rival supporters engaging in good humoured chaff and wisecracks, a quick lunch and then to Wembley.

Once at Wembley, the carnival continued. Community singing preceded the match and featured regional songs such as 'My Girl's a Yorkshire Girl', 'On Ilkley Moor Baht 'at', and 'She's a Lassie from Lancashire', as well as popular tunes such as 'It's a Long Way to Tipperary' and 'Pack Up Your

Billy Batten,
RFL secretary
John Wilson
and Harry
Sunderland

Troubles'. If the final was between teams from either side of the Pennines, neutral supporters tended to cheer for the side from their county, and informal singing competitions took place between their fans. Before the kick-off, one or two spectators often attempted to climb the goalposts and leave their club colours there. In 1930, Widnes supporter Abe Duffy amazingly managed to put his black and white cap on the top of one of the posts. This tradition carried on until the 1970s when, fearful of hooliganism, the police no longer took a benevolent view of spectators going on the pitch.

Although a majority of spectators at the first Wembley final were apparently new to the game, by the late 1930s the final had become an almost exclusively northern day out. The *Manchester Guardian* noted in 1948 that 'the crowd which came to London for the Rugby League Cup Final yesterday was much more completely Northern than for the FA Cup Final [between Manchester United and Blackpool] a week ago'. By 1951, the explanation of how league rules differed from union had been dropped from the cup final programme.

As future RFL vice-chairman Tom Ashcroft explained in 1934, winning new adherents wasn't the key point of the Wembley final:

> The playing of our Cup Final in London has never been looked upon as propaganda in the usual sense of the term, but rather to give our game a standing of national importance ... I believe we are living down the hostility and prejudice which in certain quarters operated against us and feel sure we shall win through if we insist on the game being kept clean and free from all objectionable practices.

Indeed, the fact that the day out at Wembley had become a northern event was one of its most appealing features. For many of those who visited the stadium, the combination of big match atmosphere, the celebration of northernness, and the opportunity to demonstrate the superiority of their code of rugby helped to make it one of the most memorable days of their lives, as captured in a dialect poem from Huddersfield in 1935:

> *By Gum, Fowk, it's champion. Yar Claret and Gold*
> *assembly,*
> *We've gotten into t'final, we're gooin ageean to*
> *Wembly.*
> *Tha remembers what Ah telled thi, tha knows just*
> *what Ah sed,*

*If ivver Ah got chance ageean, ther's nubdy goas
instead.*

*

*So lads, let's rally raand em, all on us do ther share,
When yo go up ta Wembly, just let em know yo're
there.
An let t'fowk know in London, dahn in yon Wembly
fold,
Ther's one teeam con play football, an that's the
Claret an Gold.*

It was Wembley stadium itself, with its military bands,
pageantry and presence of aristocracy to present the Cup,
which provided the national stage the RFL craved.

Even so, throughout the 1930s it was a common
complaint that the King never attended the final, despite
regular appearances at Twickenham. 'This continued absence
of Royal patronage to the Rugby League game is very
disheartening,' wrote a 'rugby league supporter and a loyal
subject' in 1938. 'His presence would be a great joy to his loyal
subjects in Lancashire and Yorkshire and followers of rugby
league football'. It wasn't until almost 20 years later, in 1948,
that a reigning monarch finally attended the Cup final when
George VI saw Wigan defeat Bradford, 8-3.

The Cup final carnival did not finish at the end of 80
minutes. Before the ease of coach travel allowed the sides to
return home on the Sunday, the triumphant team would be
met on the Monday evening by tens of thousands of the
town's inhabitants. The rituals surrounding the returning
victors were established in the Yorkshire Cup in the 1880s,
but now the drama was heightened by the team's long
journey from London. They would be usually welcomed at

the town hall by local dignitaries, and then the Cup would be paraded on an open-top bus through the town. The more imaginative local authorities also provided lights and fireworks. When Halifax returned home in 1931 after defeating York, twenty-two fog detonators – one for every point scored – were ignited as the train pulled into the station.

The journey from the station to the ground itself became a civic parade, as the writer Richard Hoggart remembered in his book *The Uses of Literacy*:

> I remember Hunslet rugby team bringing the Cup home from Wembley years ago [1934], coming down from the City Station into the heart of the district on top of a charabanc. They went from pub to pub in all the neighbourhood's main streets, with free drinks at every point, followed by crowds of lads prepared to risk staying out hours after their bedtime for the excitement of seeing their local champions.

In 1952, the victorious Workington Town team left their train at Scotch Corner in North Yorkshire and travelled home through the Lake District by coach.

'Every village in Cumberland turned out to cheer us home. When we reached Workington you could not get near the Town Hall, where the Mayor gave us a civic reception,' remembered Gus Risman.

As if to underline the link between a town's sporting and business success, winning sides were also sometimes presented with gifts from local businessmen. In 1931, each member of the Halifax team received a tin of Mackintosh toffee, a pipe from a local tobacconist and photograph album from the *Halifax Courier*.

83

Yet despite the game priding itself on its local links, it was rare for finalists to contain a majority of locally-born players. In 1930 and 1937, Widnes fielded twelve, while in 1934 all of the Widnes and nine of the Hunslet players were home-born. But these teams were unusual. The 1939 Halifax Cup-winning side had just a single local player, one more than their opponents, Salford. Even Keighley, the epitome of the struggling small-town team, could not muster a single home -grown player for their 1937 Wembley appearance.

Yet, there was never any suggestion that a team's success was tarnished by using imported players. In fact, as Wigan chairman Harry Lowe pointed out when he defended his club's importation policy in 1926: 'We have seven Welshmen, three South Africans, one Cumbrian, one player from the Manchester district and only one local,' going on to say that without imported players, 'Wigan would become a second or third-rate side'.

Although the 1929 crowd of 41,500 was surpassed only once before 1936, the national profile Wembley gave to the Challenge Cup final meant that the RFL decided almost immediately to repeat the experiment in 1930.

In 1931, it signed a five-year agreement with Wembley, although the 1932 final was played at Wigan because Wembley hosted England's soccer match against Scotland on Cup final day. At the RFL's 1930 annual general meeting, only one person opposed going to Wembley and, although Warrington argued in 1937 that Blackpool should be investigated as a Cup final venue, there was little serious opposition in the 1930s. This was because of the national prominence that Wembley gave the Cup final. To move back north would be seen as weakness: 'It would indicate that the Northerner was losing his grit,' argued Oldham's James Parkinson.

The only serious opposition to Wembley came from Stanley Chadwick, the Huddersfield-based supporter of the Independent Labour Party who edited the *Rugby League Review*. Chadwick argued it was the 'birthright' of rugby league supporters that the final should be in the north:

> The novelty of the thirteen-a-side code has now worn thin in the South and if future Finals are played at Wembley it will be the fans from the North who will have to pack the stadium. And how much longer are these people going to go to the trouble and expense of undertaking such a long journey to watch a match at which the only thrill is the marching of the massed bands?

Chadwick believed the game had no need to seek national recognition. He argued 'the South' had to change and pay respect to northern culture.

'If Londoners want rugby league football they must henceforth display the same enthusiasm as followers in the North,' he wrote in 1949. He saw rugby league as part of a 'true England' which was found in the working people of the industrial north and saw no reason to court national opinion. The fact that rugby league had to play its most important match in London, hundreds of miles from the homes of its supporters, was to him yet another example of the way in which the north's contribution to society was denied by the south.

However, the staging of the Cup final at Wembley was never seriously under threat.

For the RFL, a London Cup final was far more lucrative than one in the north. Even the 1954 final replay at Odsal, when, officially, 102,569 people crushed into Bradford's municipal amphitheatre, brought in less money than the previous seven Wembley finals.

Just as importantly, the Wembley ritual was immensely popular with supporters. Gus Risman pointed out that 'many people save up all the year round for the annual pilgrimage to Wembley, and they prefer to have the final played on the premier sporting arena in the country rather than on one of our grounds in the north,' and that the enthusiasm for the match was such that 'it is said that radio and television sets were mortgaged to raise money for the trip'.

Even the fact that the Challenge Cup final was usually the only major game played outside the north – only five international matches were played in London between 1930 and 1989 – heightened the sense that Wembley was a unique experience. Tellingly, the Championship final was always played in the north, allowing the most serious business of the season always to be decided in the sport's heartland.

The move to Wembley stirred strong and often conflicting emotions, but there was no doubting its success. For once, the RFL had made a controversial decision which, unusually, had pleased both the vast majority of the game's supporters and raised the game's national profile, at least for one day of the year.

9

Grassroots:
The Amateur Game's First Fifty Years

> 'We played rugby with a piece of sacking tied with
> string. As we were short of coins to toss with, the kick-
> off was determined by the leader of one team cupping
> his hand to his face and moistening one with his
> tongue. The opponents had to argue which palm of the
> hand was wet.'
> – Jack Ashley, Labour MP, 1992

In November 2012, Eastmoor Dragons reached the second
qualifying round of the 2013 Rugby League Challenge Cup.

It wasn't the first time the side had appeared in the
Cup; as any close observer of the game would know, they had
been a regular name in its early rounds throughout the 21st
Century. What was perhaps less well-known was that
Eastmoor had appeared in the very first Challenge Cup
tournament organised by the Northern Union in 1897. The
Cup was modelled on the FA Cup, so the game's leaders
invited 20 leading amateur sides into the competition to

broaden its appeal, and also in the hope that it would encourage giant-killing encounters, as happened in soccer.

They almost got their wish. Wigan narrowly defeated Radcliffe 3-0 at home, but the shock of the round came when Eastmoor were drawn at home against Stockport, one of the founding 22 members of the NU. In a strong wind, they played what the *Eastern Morning News* described as a 'stubborn game' against the semi-professionals and were drawing 0-0 at half-time. But in the second half, Eastmoor burst into the lead with an unconverted try to lead 3-0, before Stockport eventually equalised to take the tie to a replay. When the replay took place the following Wednesday, Eastmoor took an early 5-0 lead thanks to a converted try from Small, but the experience of the senior team saw Stockport take control. They eventually ran out 28-7 winners, but the tradition of amateurs pushing the professional sides to the limit in the cup was now established.

As was the case with much of rugby league, amateur sides would contribute as much to the culture of the Challenge Cup as the professional teams did.

*****

Although the formation of the Northern Union was often portrayed as a 'professional breakaway', the split was also widely supported by amateur rugby clubs across the north.

A month after the split, Hull and District Rugby Union voted 33-24 to leave the RFU and join the rebels, making them the first local amateurs to support the Northern Union. One by one local leagues and unions followed Hull's lead and abandoned rugby union.

By June 1897, there was not a single union club in the Halifax district, which was described by a local supporter of the RFU as 'a hot bed of Northern Unionism and bigotry'. At

Above: Halifax versus York in the 1877 Yorkshire Cup final

Right: Scenes from Batley's Yorkshire Cup final victory over Manningham in 1885

Below: A great ovation for Albert Goldthorpe and his team after Hunslet win All Four Cups in 1907-08. This newspaper clipping shows them touring Leeds in a decorated wagonette, with those trophies on display

Above:
A Dicky Lockwood
Baines card

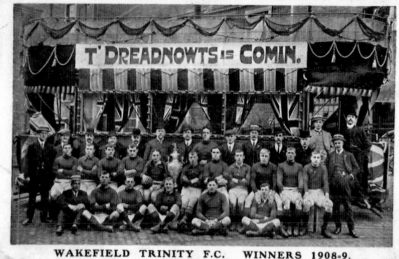

NORTHERN UNION FOOTBALL CHALLENGE CUP.

T' DREADNOWTS IS COMIN.

WAKEFIELD TRINITY F.C.   WINNERS 1908=9.

Above: Keeping it local – a postcard memento of Wakefield's 1908-09 Cup win

Left and below: Albert Henry Baskerville, organiser of the first Kiwis tour in 1907-08, and a souvenir programme from that trip

Bottom: The Northern Union line up with New Zealand ahead of their Test clash in Cheltenham

Above: A signed photograph of the great Harold Wagstaff

The GB tourists of 1920. *Back row*: Danny Hurcombe, Evan Davies, Herman Hilton, Ben Gronow, Billy Cunliffe, Douglas Clark, Frank Gallagher, Alf Wood.
Middle row: William Reid, George Rees, Arthur Skelhorne, Joe Cartwright, Arthur Johnson, Joe Bowers, Ernest Jones, Alf Milnes.
Front row: Cyril Stacey, Gwyn Thomas (vice-captain), Sidney Foster (manager), Harold Wagstaff (captain), John Wilson (manager), Jim Bacon, Squire Stockwell.
In front: Jonty Parkin, Johnny Rogers, David Murray (trainer), Joe Doyle, Billy Stone

Right:
Johnny Rogers,
Billy Batten,
Jonty Parkin

Above: Supporters assemble at Dewsbury Central Station for the trip to London, ahead of the game's first-ever Challenge Cup final at Wembley in 1929

Right: A ticket for that very match, against Wigan

Below: East Hull RFC – a rare team shot from the 1900-01 season
Pic courtesy Hull History Centre

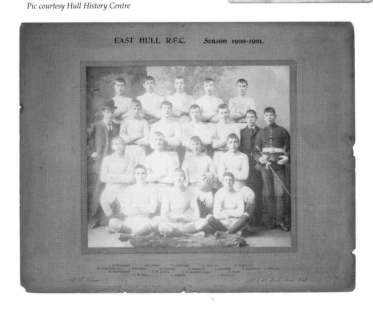

Above: The Welsh choir gathers for a photograph at Melbourne Station, during the Great Britain Lions 'Indomitables tour' of 1946

Above: Marseille is packed with jubliant people as France return from their victorious tour to Australia in 1951

Clockwise from top left: A Northern Command RL match at Halifax in 1942; an air-raid warning notice in a Wakefield v Halifax programme on 10 May 1941; RL v RU at Odsal in 1944; an advert for the Co-Op in a 1948 semi-final programme

Above: The 1946 Great Britain Lions make a media appearance at Broadcasting House, London, ahead of their long journey down under

Above: Harry Bath lifts the Cup for Warrington, after a 19-0 win over Widnes in 1950

Left: New Zealander Lance Todd, the man for whom the Challenge Cup's man of the match trophy is named

the start of the following season the *Yorkshire Post* reported that 'in Leeds, rugby union football is practically non-existent', while the NU 'is at the height of its popularity'. The Bradford and Huddersfield district rugby unions simply voted to disaffiliate from the Yorkshire Rugby Union and link up the NU. The traditional strongholds of working-class rugby in the industrial north joined the Northern Union with just as much enthusiasm as the professional clubs. By 1914, 210 amateur sides were listed in the Northern Union's *Official Guide*.

When the game was revived after the war, amateur rugby league boomed. From just 42 teams registered with the RFL for 1919-20, the number leapt to 318 in 1924-25. Growth peaked in 1929, but then fell alarmingly during the economic depression of the '30s. A 1933 report into the state of amateur rugby league stated there were no amateur clubs in Bradford, no adult clubs in the Dewsbury/Batley area, just two in Huddersfield and a mere seven in Leeds.

In 1932, Kinsley, a club based in the mining village south of Wakefield where Billy Batten was born, had debts of £40, on the verge of disbanding because 'employment [was] bad' and players had left the club to join others 'where work was better'. The depression hit so hard that even the cost of equipment could be beyond the reach of amateur sides. In December 1932, a Mr Ramsden of Halifax found his attempts to organise a team floundering and appealed to the RFL:

> We have all managed to obtain boots, socks and tights but we can see no way of obtaining shirts. ... Then there is the question of a ball. The one we at present use is patched all over and the bladder is out of a soccer ball. I feel certain that as a sportsman, you will help us to obtain both ball and shirts.

The RFL did have a policy of subsidising kit for amateur and schoolboy teams suffering hardship, although the amounts rarely exceeded £10. In February 1921, it gave fourteen amateur clubs grants of up to £5. By 1928, it employed fifteen part-time district organisers to promote the sport and organise the amateur game. It also helped with the biggest expense faced by clubs, pitch rental. This was often a massive stumbling block for clubs, as the Huddersfield & District League pointed out in its 1931-32 season report: 'Field rents are as usual the big drawback. There has not been a great difficulty in getting them but the excessive rent asked for is a very big load for clubs to shoulder. £10 for the season is as little as any owner seems to think of asking.' To help, the RFL had set up the British Playing Fields Society before the First World War as a charity to purchase pitches, but by 1930 it owned only five, one in Cumberland and two each in Lancashire and Yorkshire. Its main role was providing grants to amateur clubs so they could rent pitches, a subsidy which totalled £200 in 1930.

That wasn't the end of the cost of playing. Even when a club had a pitch and equipment, players still had to pay for insurance. Premiums could vary from 3d to 6d a match, depending on the player's age, and they would receive between ten and 20 shillings a week, usually for four weeks. This was not long enough to cover serious injuries. In 1935, Dunscroft amateur Thomas Barton was off work for four months and his compensation ran out, forcing the RFL to grant him an extra £5 to help keep his six children.

Amateur clubs also faced administrative difficulties, as was highlighted in a 1930 enquiry when a speaker from Dewsbury called the biggest one: 'committees losing interest, especially when their team was losing matches. Working men could not be expected to shoulder financial responsibility [for clubs]'. A representative from York pointed out that: '...lads who wanted to play had little money to spend on the game, and had no idea of how to raise funds or run clubs'. Financial hardship and lack of administrative experience lay behind the collapse of a huge number of clubs in the 1930s. Of the 318 amateur organisations listed in the 1924-25 RFL *Official Guide*, only 63 of them appeared in the 1934-35 edition, a survival rate of slightly less than 20 per cent.

The situation was slightly different in Cumberland, where there was no professional rugby league until 1945. Here the amateur game became the focus of civic pride. For Cumbrian towns like Egremont, Maryport and Whitehaven, playing a professional club in the Challenge Cup was almost as big an event as playing at Wembley, as a dialect poem written about Great Clifton's 1930 encounter with Keighley highlighted:

> *Clifton went ta Keighley, beat six points ta five,*
> *They landed back fra Keighley, an ivery yan alive*
> *The meade a glorious story 'at Keighley won't forgit,*
> *Thurteen Clifton heroes chock full o' Clifton grit*
>
> *Clifton com fra Keighley, just beaten bi a point,*
> *Ah bet 'at sum war riddy ta eat their Sunday joint,*
> *Wat they'll win in Cumberlandhed best be left untelt*
> *Thear's menny a slip 'twixt cup an' club, an' heeds can*
> *suen be swelt.*

This community spirit was also shown by amateur clubs across the north. Especially during the miners' industrial disputes of the 1920s, clubs organised fund-raising matches for strikers and those locked-out by the employers in 1926.

In May 1921 local Wigan side Ince All Blacks played a match to raise funds for striking miners, and in October 1926 St Helens' sides Gartons Lane and Clock Face played in aid of miners' relief funds.

The backbone of the amateur game in the interwar years was provided by supporters' clubs and work-based teams. Supporters' clubs provided administrative know-how, while works' teams benefited from sports facilities provided by companies. The Yorkshire Federation of Supporters' Clubs organised the Yorkshire Inter-Town Boys League, and supporters' clubs also took the lead in arranging local factory, or 'workshop', competitions in Batley, Bradford, Hunslet and York. Teams entered in workshop competitions tended to be scratch sides formed especially for the tournament. In 1909, 44 sides entered Huddersfield's workshop competition while 80 entered Broughton Rangers' 1911 competition. Crowds could also be sizeable. Over 10,000 turned out for the final of the Wakefield works competition in 1933, and 7,000 spectators saw the 1939 final of the Halifax Workshops tournament.

But it was the growth of company recreational facilities, such as pitches, clubhouses and even transport, that was a key factor in the survival of new amateur sides in the 1930s. By 1939, over a quarter of all amateur rugby league clubs were employer-supported factory 'works' teams. In towns with strong rugby league traditions, work-based competitions could be extensive. By 1938, the Hull Works Sports Association had more than 700 registered players, 20 teams and five different competitions. St Helens had numerous works sides, such as United Glass Bottle Manufacturers, Ravenhead Glass and the mysteriously titled Uno's Dabs. Pilkington Brothers, the town's major employers, had their own league comprising teams from different company departments.

Although they had originally been formed for the benefit of employees, most workplace teams soon dropped their commitment to selecting only players who worked for the company. Hull's British Oil and Cake Mills side, formed in 1911 and a regular in the first round of the Challenge Cup from the 1920s, quickly lost its reliance on employees, reducing the company's involvement to little more than providing pitches. Warrington's Orford Tannery works' side didn't even bother with an employee-only rule, ostensibly because the firm did not have a large enough workforce.

Whatever their level of success, all amateur clubs suffered one problem in common: the professional clubs. Although there were numerous Welsh, Australian and New Zealand players in the top flight, the vast majority of professionals learnt their trade in amateur rugby league. When a professional club signed someone from the amateur game, they were supposed to pay a signing-on fee of £10 to the players' amateur side. This rarely happened. In 1933, the Wakefield local organiser complained to the RFL that he had written fifteen letters that season to West Yorkshire clubs asking, to no avail, for the money. Such issues would continue to plague the game into the 21st Century.

Despite their grievances with the professional clubs, the culture of rugby league meant that amateur clubs and players generally behaved just like the professionals, bending the rules to their advantage and seeking victory at all costs. Although called 'amateur', many top clubs paid their players. Even before they became a professional club in 1926, Castleford paid seven shillings and sixpence for a win and five shillings for a loss. In contrast to the fanaticism of the RFU, the RFL does not seem to have policed amateurism, preferring instead to draw the line at professionals turning out for amateur sides. A 1927 cup tie between Askern Miners'

Welfare and Kirk Sandal in West Yorkshire had to be replayed when it was revealed that the Welfare team included a certain Billy Batten in its ranks, in violation of the rules forbidding professional players. It goes without saying that on the field, amateur players were no less competitive than professionals. In the 1932-33 season the Wakefield Intermediate League for players between the ages of 15 and 21 had 39 players sent off in 184 matches, a far higher rate than the professional game, which averaged around 70 players dismissed per season in the 1930s. Officials were no less competitive. In 1937, the RFL's amateur sub-committee reported that the sport was being stifled by endless complaints about the administration of the game and appeals against the results of matches.

Despite these difficulties, the amateur game strongly believed it had an important role to play in local communities. In 1925, the RFL issued *Speakers' Notes* for local organisers, point three of which was:

> To play in the true spirit of the game, and not put too much importance on the winning of matches. Cultivate the open game as this is more enjoyable to players and likely to attract more spectators. Players to support captain and committee.

Wakefield organiser Tony Bland exemplified this attitude in his dealings with young players who had been sent off during matches:

> In some cases I write a letter to the boy, and in this case not only does the boy see it but also his parents as well and this does show to them that we are out to do our best in trying to teach the boy to play the game & be a sport, and may I add that on

> more than one occasion it has been said to me that
> I was doing more good than the parson's do. [*sic*]

These attitudes were especially strong in schools' rugby league, which until the 1970s was entirely confined to boys. The fortunes of schools' rugby league fluctuated between the wars more than any other sector of the game. Most school sports were dependent on the enthusiasm of individual teachers. Unlike soccer or rugby union, there wasn't a constant supply of those with rugby league backgrounds moving from grammar schools or universities back into the education system. Moreover, no private or grammar school would have even considered playing league. A 1938 RFL survey found there were 126 schools fielding 205 teams in the towns of the eleven clubs that responded. The Leeds/Hunslet area had 39 schools and Wigan just eight, which meant, if extrapolated, that the number of schools playing the game across the north would be around 320.

Schools' finals were major occasions in rugby league towns. In 1936, 10,000 people turned out for the St Helens' schools cup final, while 5,000 did so for the Leigh tournament. Some schools, such as Hunslet Carr in south Leeds, east Hull's Courtney Street and Barrow's Risedale School, became powerhouses of the game. Between 1920 and 1939, Courtney Street and Hunslet Carr did not lose a match for ten and five seasons respectively and produced dozens of future professional players, while Risedale supplied three captains of the national team: Bill Burgess, Willie Horne and Phil Jackson.

And of course, the game was played informally outside of school. In Widnes in the 1920s, remembered future Labour MP Jack Ashley, '...we played rugby with a piece of sacking tied with a string,' in the street, the kick-off being determined by whether one team captain could guess which hand the opposing one had secretly moistened with his lips. He and his friends collected Oxo coupons to get a real rugby ball. Sadly, the ball was run over by a lorry during the first match in which it was used.

Such matches ranged from kickabouts between boys in the same street to much more elaborately organised games between teams representing several streets or districts. The Oscar-winning actor Peter O'Toole grew up in Hunslet and made a name for himself as a speedy 12-year-old in a side called Raggy-Arsed Rovers, playing teams with names like Chip Shop Wanderers and the Silly Army. As in Widnes, rugby balls were often made with patchworks of leather pieces inflated with a bicycle tyre inner-tube, rolled-up newspapers or just rags. Occasionally, an unlucky player would be forced to 'volunteer' a shoe. But, as O'Toole remembered, it made the game no less thrilling:

> Two or three matches between teams from various clusters of streets were played simultaneously. One sometimes found oneself straying into others' matches. Goalposts were a premium. If the pair had already been snatched, often a player's younger brother, 'our kid', would find himself elected as a post. Kit was irrelevant. A familiar figure with the ball, you supported him; an unfamiliar, you downed the bastard.

It was a philosophy that was as suited to rugby league as it was to the political animals of Westminster or the shark pools of Hollywood.

10

•

Into the Valleys... and Beyond

'*The Rugby League today is much too parochial.
Expansion is essential.*'
    – Fred Marsh, *Athletic News* journalist, 1923.

On 2 December 1920, the Northern Union committee discussed a letter from a Mr Thomas J Rees, the secretary of Ebbw Vale rugby union club in South Wales. He asked for an assurance that, if their members voted to switch, the club would be accepted into membership of the NU. He asked, for obvious reasons, if his letter could be kept confidential. Barely two years after the end of World War One, the game was poised to make a major breakthrough in South Wales.

However, when the NU discussed the application, it decided to reply to Rees by telling him it could not guarantee confidentiality because it had to inform its clubs about his letter. Needless to say, Rees did not pursue the matter and Ebbw Vale stayed loyal to the Welsh Rugby Union. It was not the first time – and certainly it wouldn't be the last – that rugby league had dropped the ball over the try-line.

The establishment of rugby league in Canada in 1943 was never aided by the Lions or Kangaroos playing exhibition matches there on their way back from tours, unlike touring rugby union sides. Neither the Canadians nor the American All Stars, who had toured France in early 1954, were invited to that year's World Cup. The game's International Board does not even seem to have discussed rugby league in Yugoslavia, where the game had been established in 1953, and, apart from sending rule books, there was no attempt to engage with the Romanian Rugby Union Federation after it contacted the RFL in late 1954 to find out more about the game. Frustratingly, throughout its history rugby league has had an unerring knack of never missing an opportunity to miss an opportunity.

*****

It wasn't the first time that Ebbw Vale had tried to join the Northern Union. The announcement of A.H. Baskerville's New Zealand rugby league tour in 1907 caused shockwaves throughout South Wales. Wales had been the only side to defeat the 1905 All Blacks and the prospect of another meeting with New Zealand rugby players exposed the underlying tensions in Welsh rugby union. In May 1907, E.H. Rees, a former secretary of Aberdare rugby union club, told the press he was forming a rugby league team in the town. A few weeks later, a new club was announced for Merthyr and, in July, Ebbw Vale voted 63-20 to switch codes.

Both Merthyr and Ebbw Vale were accepted into rugby league, but ended their first season in the bottom five of the league. The following season Aberdare, Barry, Mid-Rhondda and Treherbert joined. Although Merthyr and Ebbw Vale finished eighth and fourteenth in the league in 1908-09, the others struggled badly. Crippled by the costs of travelling north, hamstrung by Northern clubs picking off the cream of Welsh talent, and outclassed by experienced English teams, which meant crowds rarely rose above a few thousand, Aberdare, Barry and Mid-Rhondda folded after their first seasons, followed by Treherbert the next. Methyr struggled on until 1911 and finally Ebbw Vale, who reached the quarter-finals of the Challenge Cup in 1910, threw in the towel just before the 1912-13 season began. Rugby league's dreams of expansion into the Valleys seemed to have evaporated.

Shared culture, divided sport

Why did rugby league fail to flourish in South Wales? After all, it was also a region based on heavy industry where rugby was heavily working class. The social and playing similarities between South Wales and Northern England were recognised in the early 1880s. In 1884, Wakefield Trinity, Batley, Dewsbury and Hull visited Cardiff, Llanelli, Neath and Newport. Touring northern clubs received rapturous welcomes, as Llanelli's Elias Jones recalled:

> Hull were especially popular visitors, and I remember that the horses were taken off the coach in which they were to travel and the coach dragged to the Thomas Arms by the people who had gathered to welcome them. ... many had secured cotton waste from the works and lit this to form a torchlight procession. Arriving at the Thomas Arms, there were scenes of great enthusiasm, and the Hull captain had to make a speech from the balcony.

The first Welsh player to have 'Gone North' seems to have been Llanelli's international full-back Harry Bowen, who signed for Dewsbury in 1884 but returned home after only a few games. But the first Welshman to make a real impact was Cardiff and Wales half-back 'Buller' Stadden, who went to Dewsbury in September 1886 with his team-mate Angus Stuart. Across the Pennines, Oldham set the pace by signing Bill McCutcheon in 1888, swiftly followed by fellow international Dai Gwyn. Perhaps the most famous Welsh signings were the brilliant brothers, David and Evan James, who transferred from Swansea to Manchester's Broughton Rangers in 1892 for a reputed signing-on fee of £250, in flagrant violation of the RFU's amateur regulations.

Welsh clubs responded by offering their star players inflated expenses, known as 'boot money', and attractive jobs. The business networks of leading Welsh clubs also offered social mobility for some players, a benefit the northern clubs could not match. The Welsh Rugby Union turned a blind eye to payments to players, and this inevitably led to a head-on clash with the RFU. In 1896, the year after English rugby had split apart, a testimonial fund for the Wales captain and its greatest player, Arthur Gould was started. A brilliant three-quarter, he captained Wales to the Triple Crown in 1893, and became the first Welsh player to be a household name in the Valleys. The testimonial raised so much money the Welsh Rugby Union bought Gould's house with the proceeds and gave it back to him as a gift. The RFU declared this to be a clear breach of its amateur rules, and the Welsh withdrew from rugby union's International Board in protest. It seemed it was only a matter of time before a split took place.

But the RFU realised expelling Wales would weaken international rugby union and strengthen the Northern Union, so it decided that, although Gould was guilty of professionalism by accepting the gift, 'exceptional circumstances' meant he would not be banned. RFU secretary Rowland Hill defended the decision as 'a question of expediency' and future cabinet minister FE Smith told *The Times* the RFU had compromised to, '...prevent the great accession of strength to the Northern Union which would have followed, had the Welsh Union been driven into their arms.' The 'Gould compromise' locked Welsh rugby into the RFU's version of rugby. As long as the Welsh clubs pretended not to pay their players, the RFU would pretend to believe them. There would never again be serious confrontation between Wales and the RFU, and rugby league would forever struggle to gain a foothold in one of its natural constituencies.

Welsh rugby union benefited enormously from the Northern Union however. The 1895 split had weakened the England national side so much that between 1899 and 1909 Wales defeated England in all but one of the eleven matches they played. Even the one they didn't win ended in a draw. The Welsh ability to beat England consistently in the 1900s was vital in making rugby union the Welsh national game – a run of victories that would have been impossible if the RFU had not driven out the northern clubs.

But while the leaders of Welsh rugby union preferred to maintain its alliance with the middle-class leaders of the RFU, the same could not be said for many of its working-class players. Although we do not know how many Welsh players went north before World War One, let alone those who did before 1895, we do know that 392 Welshmen signed for professional rugby league clubs between 1919 and 1939, of whom 69 were Welsh rugby union internationals. Names like Jim Sullivan and Gus Risman, who both went north from Cardiff as teenagers in the 1920s, became some of the greatest players ever to play league, alongside numerous others who made their careers, and often their homes, in the north of England.

The inter-war years were a golden age of the Welsh rugby league player. The depression hit South Wales so hard that 430,000 people emigrated to England in search of work during the inter-war years. Those lacking rugby skills did not go to northern England, but sought jobs in new engineering and services industries of the midlands and the south east. This was one of the major reasons for the creation of new professional league clubs in London in the 1930s – London Highfield, Acton & Willesden, and Streatham & Mitcham – who hoped they would attract support from Welsh migrants now living in the South East.

The impact of Welsh players on rugby league can be seen in the numbers selected for Lions' tours to Australia and New Zealand.

Between 1910 and 1946 there were never less than six Welshmen in the touring party, with a record eleven on the 1946 'Indomitables' tour. As Robert Gate has highlighted, a Welshman played in every one of the first 110 British Test match teams between 1908 and 1958. The streak only ended because the first-choice hooker, Hull's Welshman Tommy Harris, was injured. At club level, their influence was just as great, perhaps at no time more notable than in 1937, when Keighley selected eight Welsh players for their first and only Challenge Cup final, and switched their traditional kit to the red of Wales in honour of them.

While the stereotype of the evil rugby league scout tempting young players with promises of untraceable hard cash was always central to Welsh rugby union mythology – 'When I see the jack, or the knave, or the devil I think of the rugby league scouts,' said Welsh comedian Max Boyce – the loss of talented rugby players was a self-inflicted wound. By banning 'professionals' for life, rugby union itself prevented them from returning to its game. Players went north to earn money for their rugby skills, just as their soccer and cricket-playing compatriots did. It was rugby union's amateur rules which forced players to leave Wales, as Jim Sullivan recounted:

> I was serving my apprenticeship to a boiler-maker, and I seemed to have little prospect of securing another job ... the Cardiff club would have done anything to keep me, but when I broached the subject, officials said that I could have been given a job on the ground, but that would have meant me being classed as a professional.

The ever-present risk of injury, and the hardship that could follow for the player and his family, was another powerful factor for men deciding to go north. When Bradford Northern chairman Harry Hornby went to Trevor Foster's parents' pub to sign him in 1938, the young forward initially refused, telling Hornby that he wanted to play for Wales. Hornby had already laid out £400 in cash on the kitchen table when Foster's elder sister overhead what was going on:

> She walked into the dining room where we were talking and she said, 'Mum said you're not going.' I said 'No I'm not. I want a Welsh cap.' She said 'What if you break your leg next Saturday when you play Penarth?' I picked up the pen and signed. And the greatest thing I ever did was to turn [professional] and play for Bradford Northern.

103

Rugby league offered working-class Welsh rugby players an opportunity to escape a life down the pit, in the steel works or on the dole. Some Welsh players, such as Neath's Dai Davies, who went north in 1926, even saw the union game as a showcase to secure a league contract. And once their careers had ended, numerous Welshmen settled in the northern towns where they had become stars and symbols of the community.

Going to the Dogs?

Despite the difficulties faced by rugby league in Wales, it did not dampen Welsh interest in the game. Around 13,000 spectators turned out in December 1921 to see the Kangaroos narrowly defeat the Welsh rugby league side, 21-16, at Pontypridd's Taff Vale Park.

Five years later, 23,000 saw England defeat Wales, 30-22. Not long after, some Pontypridd businessmen formed a club which was quickly accepted into membership of the RFL. As Daryl Leeworthy has pointed out, its prospects seemed bright on the surface. The local union team was struggling, its club secretary, a well-known member of the Miners' Federation, was being investigated by the Welsh Rugby Union for 'extremism', and the town's soccer team had recently disbanded.

But the economic conditions could hardly have been worse. The price of coal had collapsed and the South Wales economy was in deep depression. When Pontypridd RLFC played its first match in September 1926, miners throughout Britain had been locked out by the mine owners since May 1, and would not return to work for two more months. The RFL's South Wales organiser, John Leake, told the governing body in November that: 'Owing to 80 per cent of the surrounding population being unemployed, the gates being taken at Taff Vale Park were not quite meeting the expenses of the home and away matches'.

Things got far worse and, on 25 October 1927, just eight matches into the new season, the club resigned from the league, with debts of £1,393. Despite the professional club's collapse, rugby league did gather local grassroots support. In 1929, eight Welsh clubs applied to play in that season's Challenge Cup and the Pontypridd and District Amateur Rugby League played on until 1930, when the WRU declared an 'amnesty' for local league players.

Two months after the Pontypridd demise, a new club, based at Cardiff's recently built greyhound stadium, was accepted into the league for the 1928-29 season. But it never got off the ground and its league place was taken by a new club in Carlisle, also owned by a local greyhound racing company. Unfortunately, Carlisle United were admitted to the Football League that season too and, unable to compete, the rugby league club played just ten games before folding.

Nevertheless, greyhound-racing promoters continued to show interest in league. Part of the same boom that saw speedway and ice hockey come to Britain in the inter-war years, greyhound racing began in 1926, and drew over five-and-a-half million spectators in its first full season. By 1932, more than 20 million people watched it and greyhound promoters sought to attract other sports to use their stadia.

At the first Wembley cup final in 1929, the RFL met Brigadier-General Alfred Critchley, the managing director of the Greyhound Racing Association, to discuss creating a London rugby league club. Critchley was a Canadian who had worked on the government's strike-breaking *British Gazette* newspaper during the General Strike. His association

Another missed opportunity? The Italian rugby league magazine Gioco a XIII *of May 1961 hails a historic victory over a French side. Soon after, the game was absorbed into rugby union.*

owned the White City Greyhound Company and he wanted to bring spectators to the stadium when there was no racing.

In 1932, he purchased the struggling Wigan Highfield club. He renamed it London Highfield and from the 1933-34 season it played on Wednesday nights under floodlights at White City, averaging 6,000 spectators and finishing a respectable fourteenth in the league. But Critchley had underestimated the costs of running a professional sports team. He lost £8,000 that first season and quickly sold Highfield to the Electric Hare Greyhound Company, who moved it back north where it became Liverpool Stanley.

Six months later, the RFL received a letter from Sydney E. Parkes, the owner of Wandsworth Greyhound Stadium who said he had two stadia for teams in London. He believed he could attract northern workers who had moved to London in search of work, a view supported by a London rugby league fan:

With the transference of workers to the South during the last few years, many of whom are rugby league enthusiasts, I think that there has never been so good a chance of establishing a rugby league club as now. At Dagenham alone there are now working hundreds of former supporters of the Salford club.

The RFL eventually accepted Acton & Willesden and Streatham & Mitcham for the 1935-36 season. Parkes pulled a masterstroke by signing the All Blacks Charlie Smith, Eddie Holder and, most stupendously, George Nepia, perhaps the greatest union player in the world. But Parkes was only using league as a Trojan horse to obtain greyhound racing licences for his stadia. As soon as Acton's Park Royal stadium was granted one at the end of 1935, Parkes moved the club to Streatham's ground, which had been denied a licence. Unsurprisingly, Acton & Willesden folded at the end of the season, and Parkes put Streatham's ground up for sale. In January 1937, Parkes announced his closure of the club at the end of the season, claiming he had lost £60,000 promoting rugby league.

In Newcastle, a similar story unfolded. Newcastle rugby league club kicked off in September 1936, again based at a greyhound stadium. Four months into the season Newcastle RLFC announced that it was moving to a new greyhound stadium at Gateshead. The team won just six matches in its two seasons of existence, running up debts of £1,200 with the RFL. When it applied for re-election to the league for the following season, it was voted out by 15 votes to eight.

These new clubs failed because they were greyhound businesses which viewed rugby league as a revenue-raising scheme. When the game could no longer help dog racing they abandoned it. The perpetual struggle to sustain a professional team to which the northern clubs had become accustomed had no appeal for men like Critchley or Parkes. By mistakenly viewing rugby league as just another type of commercial entertainment, they were barking up the wrong tree.

But the small businessmen who controlled the RFL in the north saw the game as a route to local prominence, rather than a money-making venture. Except Pontypridd, none of the expansion clubs had any roots in their local communities, and these were what kept traditional rugby league clubs alive during harsh economic times. Without a rugby league team many northern towns had no presence beyond their immediate region, and their clubs embodied civic and class identities which motivated local people to keep the game alive. While money was a crucial factor in sustaining the sport, without its broader social and cultural significance the game could not survive.

Once again, rugby league was underlining how it was about much more than sport.

11
•
Rugby's French Revolution

'This is a game that will not tolerate mediocrity.'
                                                    – Jean Galia, 1934.

On Thursday 8 March 1934, Jean Galia and 16 other French rugby league pioneers held a public practice session at Headingley, in preparation for their short tour of England.

The squad was drawn from the cream of French rugby union, but they had yet to play rugby league. Their first-ever training session had only taken place at the stadium two days before, following their arrival in Leeds the previous Monday evening. That first session had been hampered because neither Jonty Parkin nor Joe Thompson, Leeds's mighty Welsh forward, spoke French. Neither could the French speak English.

It didn't really matter.

The French understood that this was how rugby should be played and quickly picked up the basics. Things were helped somewhat at the public session when a 14-year-old boy from Cockburn High School in Hunslet approached

Galia, shook his hand, and spoke to him in French, welcoming him and his team-mates to Leeds and the game of rugby league. The boy's name was Harry Jepson, who would himself play a significant role in developing rugby league in Hunslet, Leeds and around the world over his next 82 years.

The welcome that Harry and thousands of other supporters gave to Galia's Boys, as they became known, helped to convince them they had made the right decision, and they ended their six-match tour, on which they had amazingly defeated Hull, determined to ensure the success of their new game in France.

*****

Rugby had begun in France in the 1880s as a pastime for the French elite, who looked to Britain for inspiration after the national trauma of 1871, when Prussia's defeat of France was followed by the Paris Commune's revolutionary insurrection. One of rugby union's first advocates was the aristocrat Pierre de Coubertin, the founder of the modern Olympic Games, who refereed French rugby's first-ever Championship final in 1892.

The game soon became a symbol of local and regional rivalries, especially between Paris and south-west France, and was quickly embraced by all social classes.

By 1914, virtually every town and village in the South West of France had a club and big matches attracted five-figure crowds. Questions began to be asked about payments to players and a number of Welsh rugby players found jobs in French towns, which meant they could play for the local team. Rugby in the south of France began to look like the north of England before 1895.

But the French had never shared the British enthusiasm for amateurism. The great French novelist Stendhal had once said that '...who says amateur says dunce'. For their part, the RFU were always suspicious of the French. In 1911, the British rugby journalist EHD Sewell warned his readers of 'breakers ahead in the shape of possible veiled professionalism, against which the heads of the game in France must fight while the thing is still in the bud'. His fears were confirmed the following year by a Monsieur Bureau, who wrote to the Northern Union to say that 'the French clubs are run on lines which allow the payment for broken time,' suggesting that it stage an exhibition match in Paris.

The RFL had no contacts in France at that time, but immediately after the war its new secretary John Wilson, who was well-connected in the cycling world after having ridden in the 1912 Olympics, tried to stage a game in Paris with the 1921-22 Kangaroo tourists. As he probably expected, the Fédération Française de Rugby (FFR) managed to block any access to every ground in Paris, and the planned game fell through.

But as the popularity of rugby union in France continued to grow in the 1920s, so too did its problems.

Players were more or less openly paid, and moved to whichever club provided the best payment and employment package. Moreover, the balance of playing power was moving away from the elite clubs to local, more working-class teams. When a Quillan side starring Jean Galia won the French Championship in 1929 – the second of its three consecutive final appearances – it was a professional team in all but name. Based in a village at the foot of the Pyrenees, Quillan were owned by local hat manufacturer Jean Bourrel, who would become a vice-president of French rugby league in the 1930s and was the uncle of a local boy named Paul

Barrière who, aged just 27, would be elected president of the French Rugby League in 1947.

Fearful of being eclipsed by teams of a lesser social status, in January 1931, twelve top clubs left the FFR to form the Union Française de Rugby Amateur, claiming to uphold the sport's amateur values. This was followed on February 13 by England, Ireland, Scotland and Wales expelling France from rugby union's Five Nations tournament because of what they called the 'unsatisfactory state' of French rugby. The crisis had reached boiling point.

In early 1933, RFL secretary John Wilson contacted his old cycling friend Victor Breyer, who was now the editor of the Parisian paper *Echo des Sports*, and in May the RFL agreed to stage an exhibition match in Paris featuring the soon-to-arrive Kangaroo tourists. On New Year's Eve, 1933, the Kangaroos played an exhibition match against an England side at a snow-covered Stade Pershing in Paris. Australia won 63-13, but the result was irrelevant. The French crowd were amazed at the skills they had seen and carried Australian captain Dave Brown shoulder-high from the field, while the press dubbed the sport 'neo-rugby'.

Barely 48 hours later Jean Galia, under suspension by the F.F.R. for allegedly offering money to players to play for his Villeneuve-sur-Lot club, signed a contract with the RFL to bring a team to England for a four match tour in March.

In April, the Ligue Française de Rugby à Treize (LFRT) was founded. By the end of its first season it had 29 clubs, a total which ballooned to 225 in the 1938-39 season. French rugby union, which predictably tried to stop league by banning players, official and grounds, shrank to 471 in the same period. The tide seemed to be turning in favour of 'neo-rugby'.

There was widespread enthusiasm in England for the

French game. On 15 April 1934, a week after the Ligue Française de Rugby à Treize (LFRT) was founded, France hosted England at Paris's Stade Buffalo. Over 20,000 Parisians turned out to see a star-studded England side overcome Galia's men, 32-21. The following season saw the French hold England to a 15-all draw in Paris, and then win 18-11 against a Welsh team containing Jim Sullivan, Gus Risman and dual Lion Jack Morley.

The crowning moment came in 1939. In February, France beat England 12-9 at St Helens, the first time a French national rugby side had ever won in England. At the end of the season, 25,000 people watched France defeat Wales, 16-10, at Bordeaux's Stade Municipal to win their first-ever European Championship.

Off the field, France was in turmoil.

In February 1934, just as Galia's Boys were planning their first visit to England, the French parliament was attacked by armed fascists, followed by the trade unions protesting with a general strike.

In May 1936, the Popular Front coalition of socialist and liberal parties won the French elections and a huge wave of strikes took France closer to revolution. Although French rugby league was apolitical, it became associated in the public mind with the Popular Front period.

Like the millions of workers on strike, rugby league's challenge to French rugby union also seemed to threaten traditional France. The socialist minister for sport Leo Legrange was a guest of honour at a 1936 international match, and when Narbonne switched to rugby league in 1938, it was no surprise for a club whose players celebrated their 1936 championship victory by singing the *Internationale*, the communist anthem. Even if French rugby league supporters did not necessarily identify with the Popular

Front, their enemies certainly identified the 'Treizistes' with the spirit of rebellion.

Four months after France's historic victory in the European championship, France was at war. In May 1940, the German army swept across northern France. That led to a spectacular collapse of the French nation, which was divided into a German-controlled occupied northern zone, and an unoccupied southern zone controlled by Marshall Pétain's collaborationist government based in the spa town of Vichy.

France under Pétain underwent a programme of 'work, family, and fatherland,' which reasserted right-wing France's traditional values. One of those was a belief in amateur sport and so the Vichy regime banned all professional sport. But sports such as soccer were allowed to continue on an amateur basis. Only rugby league was outlawed, even as an amateur game. 'The fate of rugby league is clear. Its life is over and it will quite simply be deleted from French sport,' the minister for family and youth declared in August 1940.

On 13 October 1940, Commandant Joseph 'Jep' Pascot, Vichy's director of sport announced on national radio that rugby league would be dissolved into the FFR, and that rugby would be 'unified'. All its assets, players and clubs would be transferred to rugby union. Although rugby league ceased immediately, it was not until 19 December 1941 that Marshall Pétain issued a decree that was unique in the history of world sport: 'The association known as Ligue Française de Rugby à Treize, whose headquarters are at 24 Drouot Street, Paris, is dissolved, authorisation having been refused it'.

During the war, a number of French league players joined the Resistance. Charles Mathon and René Barnoud were active in the Sport-Libre movement, an underground organisation which opposed forced labour and the use of sport by the collaborationists.

'Rugby league is dead...' – L'Auto, 1940

François Récaborde, one of Jean Galia's 1934 pioneers to England and a founder of Pau rugby league club, was deported to the Buchenwald concentration camp in 1943. Paul Barrière played a central role in the Resistance in the Aude region.

As the Nazis retreated and the Vichy government collapsed in 1944, rugby league once again began to be played. In September 1944, Paul Barrière, on behalf of the French rugby league, met Alfred Eluère, the head of the new government's National Sports Committee, to ask for its support for the rebirth of league. He was brusquely informed that the Vichy decision would not be changed and that rugby league's assets would not be returned.

That probably came as no surprise to Barrière, because Eluère was not just a government official, he was also the president of the French rugby union.

In fact, like many institutions of post-war France, the

National Sports Committee remained firmly under the control of administrators who had been appointed under Vichy. Eventually, rugby league was only allowed under very strict conditions. It could not be played in schools, it could employ no more than 200 professional players, and it could not even be called rugby; it had to use the name Jeu à Treize (game of thirteen). The sport which had suffered the most under Vichy was treated as the guilty party.

Despite the obstacles placed in its way, the game burst back into life. Carcassonne, with 20-year-old Puig Aubert at full-back, swept all before them. They were the first champions in 1945, became the first side to do the league and cup double in 1946, and appeared in the first six Championship finals after the war, winning three.

On the international stage, France not only won rugby league's European Championship in 1949, but also achieved what the French national rugby union had failed to do in over 30 years – defeated England in England, as Puig Aubert guided his men to an historic 12-5 victory at Wembley. They were champions again in 1951 and 1952.

And then on their first-ever tour of Australia in 1951, the national side achieved legendary status. Captained by Puig Aubert, the French took the first Test, 26-15. Australia won the second Test in Brisbane, but in the final encounter at the Sydney Cricket Ground the French blew their hosts away, scoring seven tries to two, with the great scrum-half Jo Crespo claiming a hat-trick. Acclaimed as one of the best sides ever, they arrived back in France to a welcome from tens of thousands packing the streets of Marseilles. Four years later, they returned down under to repeat their success.

In 1954, the first Rugby League World Cup was staged in France, thanks to the initiative of Paul Barrière, who had originally suggested the idea in 1947. The French were clear favourites, not least because Britain and Australia had fought a hard Test series during the summer and had lost key players. But in front of 30,000 at the Parc des Princes, Puig Aubert's team were surprisingly beaten, 16-12, in the final by the wily British underdogs.

It was one of the few disappointments in Puig Aubert's career, in which he won five Championships, four cups and 46 French caps.

Nicknamed 'Pipette' because of his addiction to cigarettes – during dull matches he would allegedly loiter well behind play to have a quick smoke – he became a cultural icon of the rugby league communities of South West France. As his biographer, Bernard Pratviel, explained, his name was incorporated in everyday phrases such as the disparaging 'Hey clumsy, buy some Pipette gloves!' and the complimentary 'You have the panache of Pipette!'

However, problems were emerging for the French game. The ban on league in schools and the restrictions on professionals meant it had a shrinking pool of players to replace the Puig Aubert generation. The financial strength of rugby union could also offer far greater fiscal rewards, which meant that talented young league players were poached by the supposedly amateur game. Perhaps most notable was Jo Maso, who played amateur rugby league against England and was the son of a Carcassonne league international, but left XIII Catalan in 1962 and became one of French rugby union's all-time greats.

By the 1980s, it was not uncommon to see former professional league players turning out for French union clubs in violation of union's amateur rules, the most famous being former league internationals Jean-Marc Bourret and Jean-Marc Gonzalez. The loss of such players highlighted how far French rugby league had fallen since the 1950s. The national side reached the 1968 World Cup final and hosted the 1972 tournament, but the game lacked the financial and institutional muscle of the fifteen-a-side game. Even Test series wins against Australia in 1968 and 1978 did little to raise league's profile.

This changed in 1981, when the Championship final between Villeneuve and Perpignan's XIII Catalan gained national publicity – but all of it was negative. The match was abandoned due to incessant fighting between the two teams, leading to the sport being dropped by TV channels. The game contracted back to its roots and nursed its strong sense of injustice and defiance of the status quo.

Glimmers of hope eventually began to appear and, in 1991 the campaign for the government to replace 'jeu à treize' with 'rugby à treize' was won, although the sport's assets confiscated under Vichy were never returned. In 2006, the French game began the slow process of rebirth when Perpignan's Catalans Dragons joined Super League.

Galia's spirit had remained alive even under the toughest circumstances.

12

•

Rugby League on the Home Front

'To have survived two world wars and emerged virile was a sure indication of the strength of the rugby league movement'.
— Richard Lockwood, RFL chairman, 1946.

After a gap of more than twelve years, the Kiwi touring team arrived in Britain on 29 August 1939. It was only their third tour since Albert Baskerville's 1907 pioneers.

The second full tour in 1926 had been an unmitigated disaster. Not only did it coincide with a national lock-out of miners by the pit owners, which reduced great swathes of the north to penury, but the tour itself was wracked by a rebellion which led to players being sent home early and seven banned for life by the New Zealand Rugby League. When the 1939 tourists finally set foot in Britain, they would have been comforted by the knowledge that things could not be worse than in 1926.

They could not have been more wrong.

On September 2, they opened the tour with a victory

over St Helens – and the next day Britain declared war on Nazi Germany. The RFL scrambled to find a way back home for the tourists, and on September 14, following a last match in which they defeated Dewsbury, the tourists left on the *SS Rugitiki*, having spent just 17 days in England at an estimated cost of between £5,000 and £6,000. They were rugby league's unluckiest tourists ever.

*****

On 11 September 1939, in response to the declaration of war, the RFL suspended its competitions and set up Lancashire and Yorkshire 'Emergency Leagues'.

Unlike in World War One, there was no press campaign against professional sport in the Second World War. The RFL encouraged its clubs to support local fund-raising initiatives for war charities such as the Red Cross, St John's Ambulances and, from June 1941, 'Aid To Russia,' through collections and the staging of charity matches. RFL secretary John Wilson even offered to take a cut in his salary, although the RFL Council thought this unnecessary. Moreover, the game was seen by the government as an important factor in maintaining morale on the home front in the north, and John Wilson was made a member of the army's Northern Command Sports Board.

During the war, clubs saw themselves as community centres for supporting servicemen overseas. At Christmas 1944, Hull sent gifts to all 42 of their players in the services. Huddersfield raised £488 for Herbert Sherwood's widow and daughter after the forward was lost at sea in 1943.

As in World War One, there was no organised mourning for players killed in the war, which was such a feature of rugby union. It is even more difficult to discover how many rugby league players lost their lives in this war than in the previous one. Les 'Juicy' Adams, a veteran of the 1932 'Battle of Brisbane' Test match, was killed when the plane in which he was a gunner was shot down in the Far East in April 1945. Huddersfield also lost Ken Gronow. At least three Leeds players died: John Dixon, Oliver Morris and John Roper. Bradford were without Charles Freeman and Jack Moore. Jack Dawson and Albert Allen never returned to play again for Hull. Swinton mourned Dick Green and Tommy Holland, while Harold Briscoe did not make it back to St Helens. The most famous death occurred in England, when Lance Todd was killed in a car accident in 1942.

There may have been a war on, but controversy was never far from the surface of the game.

Shortly after the outbreak, the RFL reduced all wages to ten shillings per match. The pay cut generated uproar among players. On September 26, four days before the season kicked off, Huddersfield players led by captain Alec Fiddes said that they would not play for that amount. They were supported by Halifax and Bradford players. On October 2, representatives from almost all of the Yorkshire clubs and three Lancashire ones met to discuss their next steps. Faced with a solid front of players, the RFL Council increased payments to one pound per player, with an additional five shillings for those involved in away games at Hull or Barrow. Although not particularly satisfactory to anyone, the new terms took the wind out of the players' case and the strike threat evaporated.

By the end of the 1939-40 season, the immediate future of the game was unclear. Stadiums were requisitioned for military training or as anti-aircraft gun sites. The grounds at Leigh, Swinton, Broughton, Salford and Liverpool Stanley were all commandeered in 1940. Rochdale Hornets struggled through the 1939-40 season, before bowing to the pressures of war-time and withdrawing for the duration. They were joined at the end of the season by Hull KR. In September 1942, Hunslet supporters forced a special general meeting to overturn the committee's decision to shut the club down until the war ended. A majority voted to carry on, but financial problems meant they could not continue anyway.

By 1943, the War Emergency League, which had been formed by amalgamating the two county leagues in 1941, numbered only fourteen teams.

Clubs also suffered from rationing, introduced in June 1941. In September, the Board of Trade told the RFL that ration coupons for clothing would not be issued for playing kit but, in November 1943, it granted a special allowance to the RFL of 870 coupons, 75 balls and 150 bladders. Even so, the temptation to resort to the black market was strong. In September 1944, a Barrow official was fined £20 for illegally obtaining football clothing from an RAF officer. His barrister claimed his client was over-enthusiastically responding 'to the appeal of Mr Bevin, that the workers should be provided with relaxation, and that sport should be encouraged in every way'.

In recognition of the difficulties of travelling during war-time, the RFL allowed players to appear as 'guests' for any club that was near to work or home. This immediately boosted sides based near military camps, such as Bradford, Leeds and Halifax.

The biggest beneficiary was Dewsbury, managed by a journalist in his early 30s named Eddie Waring. Thanks to the nearby Caulms Wood army camp, where some of rugby league's biggest names were based after being called up, Waring used his considerable powers of persuasion to recruit Salford's Gus Risman, Alan Edwards and Barney Hudson,

Wigan's Jim Sullivan, Hector Gee and Charlie Seeling junior, Leeds's Vic Hey and Barrow's Roy Francis. When Dewsbury won the 1943 Championship and Challenge Cup finals, the side featured nine guest players.

It was an open secret that Dewsbury paid their guest players considerably more than the war-time maximum of 25 shillings per match. This came to light in October 1941, when the RFL investigated Wigan's complaint that Jim Sullivan had refused their offer of the maximum and opted to play for Dewsbury instead. Controversy over Waring's recruitment tactics continued to grow and, in 1943, Batley's George Smith asked: 'Who is running the Rugby League, the [RFL] Council or Dewsbury?' In 1943, the RFL discovered that Dewsbury had fielded an ineligible player in the 1943 Championship final and stripped them of the title and declared that season's championship null and void.

As in World War One, war-time 'national unity' did not lessen the competitive instincts of players, officials or spectators. In May 1940, days before the evacuation of Dunkirk, ten players appeared before the RFL Council charged with acts of violence during matches. In January 1942, Warrington's Mel de Lloyd was banned for life for punching a referee. In October 1940, a brawl between players and spectators broke out at Hunslet when spectators attacked a visiting player who punched a Hunslet one. On Boxing Day 1944, at St Helens, fans invaded the pitch to protest against a decision of the referee, and the match was abandoned halfway through the second half.

Amateur rugby league also began to re-emerge from late 1942, stimulated by the need to provide recreation for industrial workers during the long hours of war work. The Risehow-Gillhead Collieries side in Cumberland was formed to cater for the pit's Bevin Boys (young men conscripted to work in the mines). A total of 800 miners paid threepence a week to the social club, of which the rugby league side was the most prominent section. The team won two County Cup competitions and reached the first round of the Challenge Cup in 1948.

Non-works sides were also formed. Kells, in Whitehaven, was reformed in 1943 and Wigan's Pemberton Rovers were revived in 1945, thanks to the work of the Lamberhead Green Working Men's Club. By summer 1943, there were fourteen amateur leagues across Lancashire. The Halifax District League also saw nine new clubs formed due to servicemen and local men on war work. In the summer of 1944, a consortium of civic leaders and businessmen in Workington approached the RFL about starting a professional club once the war was over.

One major difference between rugby in peace and war-time was the RFU's decision, in November 1939, to lift its ban on league players temporarily, which meant rugby league players in the services could play in military and civilian rugby union games.

As in the First World War, the RFU's concession allowed its services teams to have their pick of league players. Five of the Leeds first-team were selected for the Yorkshire union side that played Lancashire at Central Park in March 1941. Leeds journalist George Thompson noted that, 'certain players, and officials too, [were] somewhat of the opinion that if they did not play [for union teams] they might jeopardise their respective positions in the Forces'. Roy Francis was a victim of this in 1942 when he was selected to play on the same day for Wales at league and England in a services union international. Despite being Welsh and a professional rugby league player, he had no choice but to play for the England union team.

Gus Risman captained both the Wales and the British Army teams in rugby union services' internationals, despite not having played rugby union since he was 17. In an early match for the British Army against the 'Army in Ireland', *The Times*' rugby correspondent commented that Irish side 'had nobody who could quite match the brilliance of Risman, the British Army's rugby league stand-off'.

In March 1942, Wales beat England, 17-12, in the first-ever services international: 'The success of Wales was largely due to their captain, A.J.F. Risman, the rugby league player, who was always dangerous in attack and very dependable in defence. He scored eight points himself and was responsible for at least one of the tries.' When the New Zealand Army tourists routed the British Army, 25-5, in December 1945, *The Times* could still single out Gus: 'Risman at right centre was brilliance itself, both as a runner and a kicker.'

In contrast, there were few opportunities to play rugby league in the armed forces. Indeed the game would not be a recognised sport in the services until 1994. Informal games were organised in Egypt, although a Rugby League XV regularly played under union rules there, and the sport was also played in German prisoner of war camps. In the spring of 1943, Stalag 383 in Bavaria organised two England versus Australia matches and a Lancashire versus Yorkshire game.

Even so, rugby league's self-confidence was boosted by the performances of its players in rugby union matches, which confirmed that league was the superior code. In March 1943, the RFL Emergency Committee minuted that league players scored 23 of England's 29 points in the victory over Scotland in a services rugby union international.

The Times noted in 1944 that England and Wales 'were ready to make use of any available rugby league talent' and numerous league players were selected for services rugby union internationals, most notably Gus Risman, who captained Wales twice, Roy Francis, capped for England seven times, and Alan Edwards, who won six Welsh caps.

Most famously, in 1943 and 1944 rugby league teams defeated rugby union sides playing under rugby union rules. In January 1943, the Northern Command Sports Board staged a union match between a Northern Command Rugby League XV and Northern Command Rugby Union XV at Headingley.

Some of the league side were former Welsh union players, but others had barely played the game. Scrum-half Billy Thornton, of Hunslet, only played his first game of union a week before. The league side won, 18-11, outscoring the previously unbeaten union side by six tries to one. The second game, between Combined Services League and Union sides at Bradford's Odsal stadium, in April 1944, was much tighter, with the League side coming from behind at half-time to win, 15-10.

A league side also won the Northern Command rugby union seven-a-side tournament in May 1943, defeating a union side of five union and two league international players. Unsurprisingly, the RFU ignored the suggestion from the secretary of the Northern Command Sports Board that there should be annual match between the two codes.

These matches were social experiments as much as they were sporting ones. The union teams comprised nine and ten officers respectively in the 1943 and 1944 sides. No officers played for either of the league sides. With the exception of Gus Risman, no significant British rugby league player of the time seems to have been appointed an officer in World War Two, highlighting how rigid the social hierarchy remained in what was claimed to be the 'people's war'. This lack of real change in society was also seen in RFU's rush to reimpose its ban on league players as soon as the war ended.

Nevertheless, there was no doubt that rugby league had a 'good war' in 1939-45. As well as its successes on the rugby field, the game's ethos of northern democratic egalitarianism fitted the rhetoric of the war years. Buoyed by this self-confidence, the RFL began its peace-time plans in the summer of 1943. Communications were re-established with the French Rugby League in late 1944 and, when the first peace-time season for seven years kicked-off in 1945, it included the new Workington Town club. A year after the end of the war, RFL chairman Richard Lockwood declared 'to have survived two world wars and emerged virile was a sure indication of the strength of the rugby league movement... rugby league was the first national game to put its house in order and play a full post-war league and cup programme'.

In 1947, reflecting its new sense of national importance, the RFL changed the name of the national side from England to Great Britain. As well as the fact the side had almost always included British players who were not English, the move was also a sign of the times, which had seen British patriotism – rather than English, Scottish Welsh or Irish – reach its height during World War Two.

At last, it seemed that society was flowing in the same direction as rugby league, and the game greeted the post-war world on the crest of a wave.

The very first issue of Rugby Leaguer

13

•

From Post-War Boom
to Post-Industrial Slump

'There are no stars in this game'.
– David Storey, *This Sporting Life*, 1960.

Few players embodied rugby league more than Willie Horne. Born in Barrow in 1922, he learned the game at the rugby league factory of Risedale secondary modern school, and then went to work at the local Vickers' shipyard where his father was employed. In December 1942, he was offered £350 to sign for Oldham, but chose Barrow, even though they paid him only £100.

He never looked back. In 1946, he was one of four Barrow players picked for the Lions' tour down under, which sailed to Australia on the Barrow-built aircraft carrier *HMS Indomitable*, and played in all three Ashes Test matches. He played in five more Tests and was captain for the victorious 1952 Ashes series. But perhaps his most sublime moment came when he skippered Barrow to victory in the 1955 Rugby League Challenge Cup Final at Wembley.

Over 66,500 spectators saw Willie control the game and kick six goals in his side's 21-12 victory. Three days after the greatest sporting moment in the town's history, he was forced to resign from his job at a Barrow steelworks after the company tried to discipline him for allegedly taking an unauthorised day off work.

The 1955 triumph sealed Willie's place in the heart of Barrow. As he told his biographer Mike Gardner, he was just an ordinary man who happened to be born with an extraordinary gift for rugby, and his story was representative of the town. Born in the depths of the post-World War One depression in the shipbuilding industry, his rise to rugby league greatness mirrored the boom experienced by the town in the decade after World War Two. When he retired from the game in 1959, the club went into a slow decline which ran parallel to that of the industry itself.

When he died in 2001, his death was announced across the front page of the *North West Evening Mail* with the headline 'RIP Town Hero and Rugby League Legend'. There could be no more fitting tribute to a player whose life perfectly reflected the game and its community.

*****

The end of World War Two saw rugby league restart with a bang. Crowds reached record levels, club finances had never been healthier, the sport had a new national prominence after touring Australasia in 1946 and hosting New Zealand in 1947 and Australia the following year.

In the 1949-50 season, total crowds at league matches were a record 4,982,160 spectators. Wigan were the most successful club in that regard, with average crowds of over 20,000 during this period and returning profits every season, culminating in a £17,000 surplus in 1950. Challenge Cup attendances also grew dramatically. In 1949, a record 846,000 people went to Cup matches, an increase of over 50 per cent on the last full season before the war. Attendances at the Wembley final ballooned to over 95,000 in 1949, and in the same season an unprecedented 75,194 crammed into Maine Road to watch Huddersfield win the Championship final. New professional clubs were formed in Workington (1945), Whitehaven (1948), Doncaster (1951) and Blackpool (1954), heralding a bright future for the game.

This affluence in an era of austerity was also seen in the rising spiral of transfer fees. In the first full season after the war, a new record transfer deal of £1,650 was set when Dewsbury brought full-back Bill Davies from Huddersfield. This was broken five times in the next two seasons, reaching a height in 1951, when Leigh purchased the ageing, yet still incomparable, hooker Joe Egan from Wigan for £5,000. Similar amounts were spent on Australian players in the two years following the war, culminating in the £12,500 that Workington offered to Clive Churchill in their unsuccessful bid to capture him from South Sydney.

The wealth of the game did not always reach the players. In January 1947, the Rugby League Players' Union and Welfare Organisation, led by Leeds's Chris Brereton, was formed. By 1950, the union claimed 800 members out of 1,300 registered professional players and had started to recruit amateur players. But in the summer of 1951, Brereton took the RFL to a government arbitration tribunal. It turned down the union's key demands for a minimum wage, a share of transfer fees and a standard signing-on fee, and the union quickly faded away.

Players also took strike action to advance their interests. In 1950, Hull players unsuccessfully struck for higher win bonuses. In 1952, all of Doncaster's players requested transfers in protest at a £2 wage cut and won a compromise £1 reduction. The following season, Castleford players refused to play Workington until losing pay was increased by a pound. Halifax players' struck for higher wages in the 1955-56 season, and the 1957-58 season began with Oldham players refusing to play unless they received £12 winning pay. None of these actions were wholly successful, in large part due to the hostile actions of club directors, but also because of the game's growing financial difficulties.

These problems were caused by the steady fall in attendances from the start of the 1950s. Crowds dipped below four million in the 1952-53 season and then fell below three million in 1959-60. Between 1950 and 1960, the average crowd at a league match halved from 9,600 to 4,829. This decline was not unique to rugby league. Soccer crowds fell by almost 32 per cent between 1950 and 1965, while cricket crowds declined by almost two-thirds from 1949 to 1960.

The RFL's initial response to the financial problems caused by falling crowds was to try to control wages.

In 1954 RFL secretary Bill Fallowfield – who had been appointed in November 1945, following the retirement of John Wilson – outlined a plan for all clubs to pay maximum match fee of £6 with no more than a £2 win bonus, but no action was taken.

Part of the problem was that professional clubs always put their own interests first. In 1959, Oldham were found guilty of making illegal loans to players of up to £600. The RFL expelled ten club committee members, forced the players to pay back the money and suspended scrum-half Frank Pitchford until he had repaid the whole of his loan. Although the club committee refused to discuss with the players when they went on strike in 1957, they were prepared make illegal payments to buy their loyalty and maintain a policy of divide and rule.

There were other financial problems too. Entertainment Tax, which had been introduced in World War One, was by 1953 raking in 16 per cent of gate takings. Insult was added to injury that year when rugby union was exempted from paying the tax, because it was amateur. The iniquity was only ended in 1957, when Entertainment Tax itself was abolished.

An even bigger issue was the poor state of most rugby league grounds, most of which had seen no investment since being opened. In 1953, Bill Fallowfield calculated that the total investment needed for vital ground improvements was over £135,000. Two years later, Halifax three-quarter Tommy Lynch argued that crowds were falling because:

> Many of the grounds leave much to be desired for the comfort of the people who make professional football possible. The paying spectator should be able to watch a match knowing that if it is wet he has a chance of being able to stand without being subjected to the weather, and not at the expense of a grandstand ticket either?

Club finances were helped in 1956 by the Small Lotteries and Gaming Act, which allowed sports clubs to organise lottery competitions to raise funds. Featherstone Rovers' profit of £2,031 in the 1962-63 season was down to their 'development fund' raising £6,007, which was almost 30 per cent of its total income. But even large amounts were not always enough.

In the 1962-63 season, Leigh raised almost £32,000 but still made a loss of £20,000. The success of these fundraising campaigns was almost entirely due to the hard work of supporters, who had become crucial in arranging raffles, weekly draws, pools, dances and bars at matches. In 1955, Featherstone supporters' club spent £2,300 on building new dressing rooms and improving terracing. The following year, Halifax received £4,500 from their supporters' club. Players' testimonials were also organised by supporters. Between 1945 and 1970, Huddersfield supporters' club raised over £12,500 for 14 players.

Nevertheless, attendances continued to fall and the game lost one-and-a-half million spectators between 1959 and 1964. The split of the league championship into two divisions in the 1962-63 season – a change demanded by many clubs at different times since the 1920s – did not halt the decline. But the clubs panicked in 1964 and reverted back to one division, which also did nothing to increase attendances.

The crisis facing the game was demonstrated by Bradford Northern's collapse in 1963. A decade earlier, Odsal's average crowd was 17,169, but in 1963 it had dropped to just 1,257. On 23 November 1963, just 324 people saw the game against Barrow and the next month the club withdrew from the league with debts of over £11,000. As usual, it was supporters and the local community that brought Northern back to life.

In January 1960, the RFL had held the first of many discussions about the game's decline and, very slowly, things began to change. In December 1967, professional clubs began to play Sunday matches – which amateurs had been doing since 1954 – and most clubs soon abandoned the traditional Saturday afternoon for Sundays or, if they had floodlights, Friday nights. Substitutes were allowed for the first time in 1964 and the four-tackle rule was introduced in 1966.

The showcase for these innovations was the Floodlit Trophy. Begun with just eight clubs in 1965, on the initiative of BBC2 controller David Attenborough, the RFL encouraged support for the tournament by offering loans to clubs for the installation of lighting. Only Bradford and Leigh had floodlights before 1965, but over the next two years 17 clubs installed them. The competition became a staple of BBC2's Tuesday night programming until the channel withdrew its support in 1979.

The Floodlit Trophy was the least controversial aspect of rugby league's relationship with the BBC. Problems began as soon as the Corporation first broadcast the sport with EG Blackwell's commentary on the Oldham versus Swinton Challenge Cup final in 1927. That December, the RFL Council wrote to the BBC complaining that rugby league results were not read out with soccer and rugby union scores on the Saturday tea-time news. The RFL made exactly the same complaint in 1948. 'Many of us in the North have a suspicion that someone with an 1895 complex rules in a high place at the BBC,' protested the Huddersfield Supporters' Club in 1946, and in 1951 the *Rugby Leaguer* organised a 25,000 name petition calling for scores to be read out. The following year, RFL secretary Bill Fallowfield noted, '...there is no doubt that the public are not happy with the commentaries on rugby league which are made either on TV or sound broadcasts.'

This was not paranoia. Asa Briggs, the historian of the BBC, noted that rugby league 'was treated very cautiously as a socially inferior local sport.' Drawn entirely from the public and grammar schools, most BBC sports broadcasters in the 1930s had little knowledge of league.

In September 1933, the BBC considered broadcasting commentary of London Highfield's matches, but felt obliged to ask the RFU if it 'would regard with disfavour' such broadcasts. The RFU had unsurprisingly said that it would, and because the BBC 'did not wish to in any way alienate the Rugby Union', the proposal was dropped. More generally, the BBC's attitude to rugby league was a symptom of its wider inability to engage with working class people without being condescending. These problems came to the fore with the arrival of television.

The BBC televised its first live match in 1948, strangely restricted to the Birmingham area, and in the 1951-52 season it broadcast four games nationally, including the Cup final. But in 1953 the RFL refused permission to televise the decider because it believed live coverage affected the 1952 crowd, which was 22,000 lower than it had been in 1951. For the next two decades the game was riven by suspicion of live TV coverage and the conflicting desire for publicity. During the 1960-61 season, Warrington lobbied successfully to stop live TV coverage. Contrary to expectations, attendances fell but rose when the cameras came back. This didn't convince everyone and, in 1965, Wigan were fined £500 by the RFL for refusing to play a televised Cup-tie and, in 1969, Warrington tried to organise another campaign against live TV.

But by then, the game was relying on television money to stay afloat. In 1964, the BBC paid £31,423 for broadcast rights. In 1967, it paid £200,000 over three years and extended for another four years in 1970. As the RFL's negotiating team explained, it was difficult to 'see how clubs could hope to obtain an average of £4,000 per annum or more for four years from any other source'. And if the game accepted the BBC's money, it also had to accept the BBC's presentation.

In January 1973, the RFL protested to the BBC that 'rugby league was being used and games were only being televised when nothing better could be found, rugby union matches being preferred at times, and rugby league always seemed to be hit when very early kick-offs were required ... [sometimes] simply to show a western film.' There was also the problem of the commentator.

Eddie Waring had been the BBC's rugby league commentator since 1951, and became a household name in the 1960s. His commentary style was criticised as early as 1952 and complaints grew stronger as the game's fortunes fell and Waring's fame rose. His response to Don Fox's last-minute conversion miss that would have brought the Challenge Cup to Wakefield in 1968 – 'he's a poor lad' – was heartfelt, but reduced a moment of epic Greek tragedy to the level of a *Coronation Street* script. Whether intentionally or not, Waring fulfilled the BBC's stereotype of the north, and this was exactly what appealed to many of Waring's supporters outside of rugby league.

Geoffrey Mather of the *Daily Express* claimed that Waring's 'lips [were] equipped with tiny clogs', while the *Daily Mail*'s Ian Wooldridge argued that his image 'was all about slagheaps, Tetley's ale, black pudding, Lowry paintings, busted noses'.

In fact, Waring's on-screen persona was a form of minstrelsy which fulfilled the stereotype expected of him, but it did not reflect his talents or intelligence.

As a journalist, he was a pioneer of the pugnacious sports journalism which emerged in the 1950s and 1960s. His writings are full of passion for the game, its history and its culture. More than any other journalist, he promoted rugby league's egalitarian ethos: 'For years I have been plugging rugby league football as being the most democratic game in the world,' he told his readers in 1948. But rugby league's weakness in the 1960s meant that Waring's TV appearances on *It's a Knockout* and the *Morecambe and Wise Show* gave him a higher profile than the game itself. And when people laughed at him, it seemed to many in the game that they were not laughing with him, but at the north and rugby league itself.

137

The issue came to a head in 1971, when the RFL appointed marketing consultant John Caine to examine the problems facing the game. Caine's report said the BBC's presentation was 'totally detrimental to the life of the game'. Waring's commentary was described as 'unfortunate' and his humorous style criticised because, 'the laughter is patronising and lends support to the view of rugby league held by midland and southern watchers'. As usual when criticised, the BBC became more intransigent and refused to discuss the issue. In 1976, the 1895 Club, formed by supporters based in St Helens to campaign on behalf of the game, presented an 11,000 strong petition to the BBC calling for improved coverage and heavily criticising Waring. The BBC took no notice and Eddie, clearly struggling due to age and what would later be diagnosed as dementia, carried on commentating until his retirement in 1981.

The power that TV now had over the fortunes of the game was one of the more obvious signs of the deep social changes undermining rugby league. By 1961, 75 per cent of households had a television; ten years later the figure was 91 per cent. Car ownership also leapt from 2.3 million in 1950 to 11.8 million in 1970, and home ownership also grew from 16 per cent of all housing in 1945 to 47 per cent in 1970. Leisure became more individual and less collective, as could be seen in the fate of cinema, where admissions dropped by 87 per cent between 1946 and 1970. Pubs and Working Men's Clubs also closed at an unprecedented rate.

Similar social changes took place in Australia and the United States, yet in those countries rugby league and professional gridiron reached new heights of popularity thanks to television. What lay at the heart of the game's problems in the North of England was the decline of its industrial heartlands. By 1970, over two-thirds of all coal mines had been closed since the end of the war. The number of dockers fell by almost a half between 1951 and 1971, with those in Hull declining by a third. In 1954, 735,300 people were employed in the textile industry, but by 1984 there were only 74,400. At the same time, slum clearances and new out-of-town housing estates saw significant population decline in many traditional rugby league areas. For example, between the 1951 and 1981 censuses, the population of Bramley fell by 15 per cent, while that of Hunslet dropped by over a half.

At the same time, the importance of regionalism was declining, as Britain became more centralised and nationally-focused, as seen by the *Manchester Guardian* dropping Manchester from its title in 1959 and eventually moving to London in 1970. By the 1970s, the production of regional editions of national newspapers was ending. Televised sport meant people didn't even need to live in the same city as a club to be a supporter of a soccer team like Manchester United or Arsenal. Conversely, clubs in smaller regional towns lost much of their national importance. This falling interest in regional contests could be seen in the Lancashire versus Yorkshire cricket rivalry. In 1954, 30,818 watched the Roses match at Headingley. By 1978 the attendance was 7,229. Rugby league was hit hard by these trends.

These changes in society shifted what it meant to be northern and working class in the 1960s. This was highlighted in David Storey's 1960 novel, *This Sporting Life*. Born in Wakefield in 1933, Storey won a scholarship to the local Queen Elizabeth Grammar School. After leaving, he both studied at London's Slade School of Fine Art and played rugby league for the Leeds 'A' team. The novel describes the ultimately tragic relationship between league player Arthur Machin and his widowed landlady Valerie Hammond. Its depiction of rugby league is not flattering. Machin describes how he is 'knocked about, thumped, cut, and generally treated like a piece of mobile refuse, just so that I could have that extra load of cash.' Rugby league, he says, is a 'game played for money, personal prestige, and an enjoyment composed of these two and other elements, [in which] the animal fills most of the ranks.'

The film adaptation of the book premiered three years later. Directed by Lindsay Anderson and dominated by Richard Harris's Brando-esque portrayal of Machin, the film was a major success, with Harris being nominated for an Oscar. But the film was not welcomed by everyone. Hull KR supporters' club complained that the film was 'detrimental to the rugby league code', and reviewing the film for the *Rugby Leaguer*, Ray Fletcher (using the pseudonym Ramon Joyce) said: '...my worst fears of the film... were unfortunately realised.'

This Sporting Life presented rugby league as deeply out of step with the changes of the 1960s and the fashionable young north epitomised by the Beatles and actors like Salford-born Albert Finney and Hull-born Tom Courtenay (who was actually a Hull FC supporter). Rugby league's northernness seemed to be rooted in history. The game's imperviousness to a changing world and inability to escape the past were evocatively captured by Arthur Hopcraft in a 1964 article for the *Sunday Times Colour Magazine*:

> There is an extraordinary anachronism about the setting of League, its grounds bounded by the living museum pieces of the heyday of British heavy industry; a railway line on one side, the eyeless wall of some tired-out old mill, the colour of dried blood, on another, and behind you the

bent backs of the terrace rows, built in brutal meanness for men with fears and families; and from their chimneys the soot brushes your forehead like a kiss from a corpse ... Rugby league men give the impression that they know they are tethered somewhere back in the social evolution.

As the post-war world disappeared from view, the future of rugby appeared to be bleak. By 1970 attendances seemed to be in free-fall, the amateur game was collapsing, and the television presentation of the game resembled that of music hall. Few raised much of an argument against the verdict passed that year by Hull KR director Ron Chester: 'To say the game is dying is ridiculous. It's dead'.

RULES AS TO
PROFESSIONALISM

The Rugby Union Committee deem it advisable, as the game spreads in all parts of the country, to draw the attention of all players to these rules.

THE PRINCIPAL RULES AS AFFECT THE INDIVIDUAL ARE AS FOLLOWS:—

1. Professionalism is illegal.
2. Acts of Professionalism are:—

   Asking, receiving, or relying on a promise, direct or implied, to receive any money consideration whatever, actual or prospective, any employment or advancement, any establishment in business, or any compensation whatever for:—

   (a) Playing football or rendering any service to a football organisation (provided however, that the Secretary and Treasurer of a Club who has definitely ceased playing football may be excepted under special conditions).

   (b) Training, or loss of time connected therewith.

   (c) Time lost in playing football or in travelling in connection with football.

   (d) Expenses in excess of the amount actually disbursed on account of reasonable hotel or travelling expenses.

   Playing for a Club while receiving, or after having received from such Club, any consideration whatever for acting as an official, or for doing or having done any work about the Club's ground or in connection with the Club's affairs, unless such work was done before the receiver became a football player.

   Remaining on tour at his Club's expense longer than is reasonable.

   Giving or receiving any money testimonial. Or, giving or receiving any other testimonial, except under the authority of this Union.

   Playing on any ground where gate money is taken:—

   (a) During the close season (that is between 21st April and 1st September, except when the Tuesday in Easter Week falls later than 21st April, when the close season shall commence from the Wednesday in the Easter Week), except where special permission for the game has been granted by this Committee.

   (b) In any match or contest where it is previously agreed that less than 15 players on each side shall take part (except where, in exceptional cases, this Committee may have granted special permission for less than 15 players aside to take part).

   Knowingly playing with or against any expelled or suspended player or Club, or with or against any professional player or Club.

   Refusing to give evidence or otherwise assist in carrying out these rules when requested by this Union to do so.

   Being registered as, or declared a professional, or suspended by any National Rugby Union or by the Football Association.

   Playing within 8 days of any accident for which he has claimed or received insurance compensation, if insured under these rules.

   Playing in any benefit match connected with football (except where this Committee has given permission for a *bona fide* charity match).

   Knowingly playing or acting as referee or touch judge on the ground of an expelled or suspended club.

   Receiving money or other valuable consideration from any person or persons as an inducement towards playing football.

   Signing any form of the Northern Union (Rugby League).

   Advocating or taking steps to promote Northern Union (Rugby League) or other professional football.

The penalty for breach of these Rules is suspension or expulsion. (Expulsion carries with it the formal declaration of professionalism).

This Union shall have power to deal with all acts which it may consider as acts of professionalism and which are not specifically provided for.

October, 1924.   *BY ORDER OF THE COMMITTEE.*

IGNORANCE OF THE RULES IS NO DEFENCE.

14

•

Union against League: Rugby's Cold War

'The strictest form of apartheid – between rugby union and rugby league'.

– Danie Craven,
South African Rugby Board president, 1985.

Unlike almost every other player in this book, Bristol's Tom Brown never played rugby league and never even so much as set foot inside a rugby league ground. He did not even see a rugby league match until he bought his first television in 1954. His game was rugby union, in which he rose to prominence as Bristol's full-back in the late 1920s, and won the first of his nine caps for England in 1928.

Yet on 7 November 1933, Tom Brown – the man with the same name as the hero of the book that helped launch rugby in the nineteenth century – was banned for life from rugby union by the RFU. His crime? To have met with officials from a rugby league club and to allow them to pay his travel expenses.

Tom Brown's case was just one of countless other examples of persecution and discrimination by the rugby union authorities against players who simply sought to exercise their right to play sports of their choice. Union's self-righteous belief in its moral superiority ruined careers, turned officials into persecutors, and brought fear to the minds of countless players. Its paranoia about rugby league knew no bounds, and it would poison rugby for well over a century.

*****

Rugby union's attitude meant that, ever since 1895, rugby league had to cope with a situation unique in the history of sport. Union actively conspired to prevent people from playing league by forbidding its players having any contact with it, by ostracising its own players who tried the league game and by portraying league as an alien, mercenary activity, an 'incubus' even.

The RFU waged its war against rugby league through its 'Rules as to Professionalism'.

These began with the uncompromising statement that: 'Professionalism is illegal' and defined it as 'asking, receiving, or relying on a promise, direct or implied, to receive any money consideration whatever, actual or prospective; any employment or advancement; any establishment in business; or any compensation whatever.' Anything not explicitly banned was covered by section eight – 'this Union shall have power to deal with all acts which it may consider as acts of professionalism, and which are not specifically provided for.'

The RFU's rules deliberately created an atmosphere of paranoia. Posters were distributed to union clubs from the 1920s to the late 1950s, outlining 17 different ways rules could be broken. Two were outlined in thick bold type: 'Asking for or receiving any form of remuneration for playing' or 'signing any form of the Northern Union (Rugby League).' The final line of the poster ended with an ominous warning: 'Ignorance of the Rules is no Defence.' Anyone who broke these rules was banned not only from playing rugby union for life, but also from any other type of involvement in it.

The word professional was applied to all forms of rugby league, amateur or professional. It was illegal to sign any rugby league form, play with or against a rugby league player or 'advocate or take steps to promote' rugby league, whether money was received or not. Although the RFU claimed its rules covered all professional sports they only ever applied to one sport, as a 1958 International Board resolution explained:

> Persons who are or have been associated in any capacity with a Rugby League club should be regarded as being ineligible to participate in the affairs of Rugby Union clubs or teams. The Board also agreed that ... there is in general no objection to persons who are or have been ranked as professionals in games other than Rugby League football being permitted to play Rugby Union football or to participate in the affairs of rugby union clubs.

Semi-professionalism in France, Italy and Romania was openly tolerated by the International Board. In 1956, former Welsh captain and judge Rowe Harding explained to a Foreign Office official that the rugby union authorities would not expel Romania for paying its players because: 'I have no doubt that the Romanians will turn to rugby league, which will be a tragedy'.

In private, RFU committees spent considerable time discussing rugby league. In the 1920s, 'professionalism' was on the agenda for 22 of the RFU's first 30 committee meetings after the end of World War One. In 1920, Lieutenant-Colonel A. Brown was refused permission to play union because, when he was 18, he had played amateur league. In 1928, a player called Armstrong from Seaton in the North East signed for a league club. He quickly changed his mind and sent his contract back to the league club asking to be released from it. He then informed the RFU of his actions, which promptly banned him for life.

Schools were a constant source of anxiety for the RFU. In 1935, a 19-year-old schoolboy called Drinkhall was banned because he played league outside school when he could have been playing union at his school. The following year ex-RFU president James Baxter wrote to the government's Board of Education complaining that teachers were forced to teach rugby league and asked that the Board rule on what sports were played in schools, implying that league should be banned. The Board replied that sport was a matter for individual schools.

After the Second World War, the RFU Committee constantly discussed league, including reports about it in the Army, the Midlands, Surrey, and even Canada. In the summer of 1947, Ilkley RUFC asked if the incoming New Zealand rugby league tourists could use its pitch for training. Permission was denied. That same year, the RFU created the Northern Counties sub-committee (NCSC), to investigate accusations of professionalism in the north of England. In 1951, it cross-examined a young Orrell player, J.F. Hurst, three times before he finally confessed he had played ten matches for Wigan's 'A' team. That same year, a tip-off that a union player worked at the RFL headquarters in Leeds resulted in a letter being sent to Bill Fallowfield demanding to know, without explanation, whether the player, Peter Gaunt, held an executive position. Fallowfield told them he was only a clerk and Gaunt escaped a ban.

In 1962, the RFU formally banned ex-league players from becoming non-playing social members of rugby union clubs. A single advertisement in a Durham newspaper inviting players for a trial with a rugby league club in 1968 was discussed at the RFU's executive committee under the agenda title of 'Rugby League Infiltration'. Some clubs, especially in the north, even asked applicants for membership to declare that, 'I have not taken part in rugby league football, either as an amateur or a professional, nor have I signed any rugby league form, after reaching my eighteenth birthday.'

Just as in the 19th century, social snobbery was the source of the RFU's paranoia. In 1924, RFU Committee member FC Potter-Irwin said openly that, 'Rugby football [by which he meant union] was never intended as a recreation for those to whom nature has denied the high privileges of gentlemanly instinct.' James Baxter, the manager of the 1930 British rugby union tour of Australasia, told journalists that 'every town must have its sewer,' when asked why league was so popular in Auckland. The journalist TH Evans Baillie criticised league in 1949 for relying on, '...the manual-labour type who, while strong and fit enough to learn technique, is often, though by no means inevitably, liable to fall short on tactics.' Most notoriously, in 1985, South African rugby union president Danie Craven proudly called union's attitude to league 'the strictest form of apartheid.'

The RFL's response to such vitriol was by and large to ignore it. Shortly after becoming RFL secretary, Bill Fallowfield exposed French rugby union's recruitment of league players, most notably the former Toulouse treiziste Yves Bergougnan, who played for France in the 1948 Five Nations, but public silence was largely the RFL's position until the 1980s. There were complex reasons for turning the other cheek. For all its northern self-confidence, the RFL was deferential to those of a higher social class. Direct confrontation with rugby union would be seen as challenging the accepted social order. The game also felt it occupied the moral high ground and did not need to fight – not only was it a better game to play, but it also saw itself as democratic and meritocratic, in comparison to union's exclusivity.

Stories about union's discrimination helped to bolster league's sense of moral superiority. Examples of league people being banned from union clubhouses or players banished from union teams for playing league were commonplace. One of the most famous stories concerned WB Wollen's painting 'The Roses Match'. Based upon a Yorkshire versus Lancashire match at Bradford in 1893, it was widely thought that players who'd joined the Northern Union in 1895 had been painted out. This was not the case – almost every player in that match went on to play for NU clubs – but the myth confirmed the prejudices of union to league supporters.

It was the formation of the British Amateur Rugby League Association (BARLA) in 1973 that sparked the first concerted campaign against union's discrimination – and for what was called a 'free gangway,' to allow amateur players to play both sports. BARLA's Maurice Oldroyd calculated that the best way to force the RFU to change was to exploit the contradiction between the Sports Council's 'Sport For All' slogan and the significant public funds it provided to the RFU despite union explicitly being a sport not open to everyone.

The Sports Council's first response to Oldroyd was to defend the RFU's policy and send a private letter to Robin

Prescott, the RFU secretary, warning him that 'it seems quite possible that Mr Oldroyd will go to the press.' Oldroyd did just that, and also recruited MPs to challenge the Sports Council's policy. Under public pressure, the Sports Council pressed on the RFU to moderate its position. BARLA's growth in the late 1970s and early 1980s was also becoming a cause of concern for the RFU. In December 1983, it even convened a special meeting to discuss BARLA. Eventually, in April 1987, the RFU grudgingly allowed amateur rugby league players to play rugby union.

Even so, union players could still be barred from playing amateur league. And the lifting of the ban did not apply to professional rugby league. In 1993 Wasps' full-back Steve Pilgrim was banned by the RFU for a year for playing in an unpaid trial game for Leeds. A year later, Ady Spencer was stopped from playing for Cambridge University in the Varsity match after the RFU discovered that he was also a league player. But by this time the RFU was fighting a war on several fronts. In 1993, Stuart Evans, the Neath and Wales prop who signed for St Helens in 1987, took legal action against the Welsh Rugby Union accusing them of restraint of trade because he was banned from returning to union. The Inland Revenue also began to investigate unpaid tax on rugby union players' secret earnings. In 1994, Labour MP David Hinchliffe introduced his Sports (Discrimination) Bill, which sought to outlaw union's discrimination against league. At the same time, the Ministry of Defence ended its ban on rugby league in the armed forces.

Finally, under intolerable pressure from its Southern Hemisphere countries, union's International Rugby Board took the momentous decision to legalise professionalism on 27 August 1995, 99 years and 363 days since the formation of the Northern Union. The formal barrier that separated the two games had been removed, leading to speculation that they would merge. Such fears were extinguished by the Wigan versus Bath 1996 'Cross-Code Challenge', when Wigan demolished Bath, 82-6, under league rules but then lost, 44-19, playing union. Perhaps more instructive was Wigan's easy victory in that year's Middlesex union sevens tournament – a triumph repeated by Bradford in 2002 – which demonstrated that league was clearly superior in the skills common to both codes.

But if the old certainties of the oval world had disappeared, it proved more difficult for the old prejudices to go the same way. The social gulf between the codes remained as wide as ever. Although the RFL's deal with Rupert Murdoch seemed to deprive league of its moral high ground over union, this feeling was eased by union's no lesser dependence on Murdoch television money.

Rugby union's use of league players, coaches, tactics and rules also demonstrated that league was higher up the evolutionary chain of rugby. And few fans wanted the game to draw closer to union. The RFL's use of Twickenham for the Challenge Cup final in 2001 and 2006 was unpopular with supporters, while Leeds's attempt to persuade league fans to watch similarly-owned Leeds Tykes by staging a double-header with the Rhinos was greeted by protests, including a streaker who ran the length of the pitch to demonstrate his naked opposition to union.

Moreover, the marginalisation of league by the national media intensified. 'Great game, rugby league, such a shame it has to die,' wrote the *Guardian*'s Frank Keating in 2001, at the height of union's post-professionalisation hubris.

Even two decades after union had embraced the professionalism it had denounced league for, the thirteen-a-side game was still looked down on and suffered obstructions large and small from union. In Italy and South Africa, rugby union officials sought to prevent governmental recognition of league, while in 2015 rugby league pioneer Sol Mokdad was arrested and jailed in Dubai in part for his role in setting up rugby league in the United Arab Emirates.

Rugby's cold war may have ended, but its battles continued to be fought.

The Leigh Miners Welfare team which lost 12-16 to Warrington in 1976

15

•

Beyond the Professionals

'Babies don't toddle there [in Newton le Willows], they sidestep. Queuing women talk of 'nipping round the blindside' The game provides our cultural adrenalin. It's a physical manifestation of our rules of life: comradeship, honest endeavour and staunch, often ponderous, allegiance to fair play.'
— Colin Welland, qualified schools rugby league coach and Oscar winner, 1979.

Although as a young man he played for Holmfirth's Underbank Rangers, the same club as Harold Wagstaff, Maurice Oldroyd was never going to reach the heights of its illustrious roll-call of great players. His talents lay elsewhere.

In 1963, he retired from playing aged 28 and became a referee. But his real skill was as an administrator, where his organisational abilities, indefatigable spirit and passion for rugby league allowed him to shine. In 1973, when amateur rugby league was on its knees, he and Tom Keaveney founded the British Amateur Rugby League Association. It

Rugby League A People's History

flourished, and under Oldroyd's leadership, the amateur game had never been healthier. He began the campaign that led to a free gangway between the two rugby codes, and built links for amateur rugby league across the world.

Like John Wilson, the man who led the RFL from 1920 to 1945, Maurice Oldroyd was one of the few people whose work off the field decisively changed league in the same way that Wagstaff and other immortals changed the game on it.

*****

Amateur rugby league was invigorated following the end of World War Two, just like the professional game. In 1949, Leigh chairman James Hilton looked to the future with the rallying call: 'We all believe it to be the greatest game on earth. We steep in its glorious traditions and its very character comprising speed, virility and attractiveness ... we believe that if it is presented to a wider public in the right setting, it cannot fail to capture the interest.' Amateur rugby league seemed to be the natural route for the expansion of the game.

In May 1947, a 'London Rugby League Supporters' Association' was formed to promote the game in the capital. Harry Sunderland declared he would help them form 'a London working-class rugby league team of thirteen amateurs' to play against the forthcoming French amateur touring side. In the same month, Barrow played Leigh in three missionary games in Cornwall, although small crowds quickly ended the experiment in the South West. Three months later, Sunderland was offered a three-year contract to be the RFL's full-time London organiser but, when he was told he would have to give up his journalism, his fervour for expansion dried up. The post went unfilled.

Even so, at the start of the 1948-49 season the London

154

Amateur Rugby League kicked off with teams from Brixton, Mitcham and the Third Regiment of the Grenadier Guards, later to be joined by clubs in Slough and Southampton. The London league lasted until 1953, handicapped by its distance from the game's amateur heartlands and the active hostility of local rugby union. Members of the Grenadier Guards team were all disciplined by their regiment for daring to play rugby league. Organisers had hoped that industrial migrants from the North and Wales would support the game in London, but the deep roots of soccer offered integration into local communities that league could not provide. Moreover, unlike the South West and parts of the Midlands, there was no working-class support for rugby in London.

This was obviously not the case in South Wales, where hopes for rugby league expansion were more realistic. Indeed, Welsh rugby union in the late 1940s was troubled by the perceived threat from league. The Wales versus England league international at Swansea in November 1945 attracted 30,000 people, while around 20,000 saw each of the next two internationals.

At the Welsh Rugby Union's annual general meeting in 1950, former Welsh captain Rowe Harding declared that 'rugby league is only an infant, but it wants strangling.' His concerns were not groundless; 400 people attended a meeting to form an amateur rugby league club in Neath in March 1949. A few days later, the RFL appointed a full-time Welsh organiser, allocated a budget of £1,000 to Welsh efforts and arranged for Huddersfield and St Helens to play three exhibition matches. At the start of the 1949-50 season, a new Welsh amateur league kicked off with eight teams.

Unfortunately, the problems that had afflicted Welsh rugby league clubs before World War One soon reappeared. Even before the 1949-50 season began, the new Welsh clubs complained to the RFL that northern clubs were poaching their best players. Even worse, they also reported that Welsh union players were refusing to sign for local league clubs, preferring to wait until they got better offers from a richer northern club. Eventually it was agreed that a northern club signing a Welsh league player would pay £120 to his club and £80 to the Welsh league. This did little to staunch the flow north and in December 1949 the Welsh called for a ban on northern clubs signing Welsh union players. Unsurprisingly, this was rejected and instead it was agreed that the Welsh league would receive £300 every time a union player went north. There is no evidence that any club ever paid up.

The other problem for Welsh league sides was that although the Welsh public would flock to see the top league sides, they were considerably less keen on watching local amateur clubs. To overcome this, in 1951, the RFL invited the Cardiff and Llanelli league clubs to join as professional sides. Only Cardiff had the resources to do so, but the jump in standards proved too much and they won just five of 36 matches in 1951-52. Struggling financially with the demands of professionalism, the club resigned from the league at the end of the season. By this time Welsh rugby union had also recovered its self-confidence, not least because of its Grand Slams in 1950 and 1952, and the window of opportunity of the immediate post-war years that league had was closed.

In the north of England, post-war optimism meant that by 1949 there were 352 registered amateur clubs, the highest number ever.

Amateur clubs also defeated professionals twice in the Challenge Cup. Led by miner Tommy Fox, the father of Neil, Don and Peter, who were all later to their considerable mark on the sport, Sharlston Rovers defeated Workington 12-7 in 1946, while Risehow and Gillhead beat Keighley 10-2 in

1948 – the first time this had happened since Beverley won against Ebbw Vale in 1909. In 1952 Warrington's Rylands Recreation drew 9-9 with Whitehaven.

But this golden age of amateur rugby league began to fade in the 1950s.

The gradual withdrawal of large companies from employee sports provision, which began in the mid-1950s and resulted in a decline in works-based sides, increased the administrative burden on local clubs and leagues. By 1970, only Hull and Leeds still had works-based leagues. By 1964, the number of amateur clubs had fallen by a third from its 1949 total, and the game appeared to be going the way of the industries that had supported it.

Amateur rugby league was also affected by broader changes in society, especially those caused by the 1944 Education Act.

The problem had first been identified in a 1954 report on schoolboy rugby league in Cumberland, which noted that academically bright boys who had played league at primary school or for a local club were being lost when they passed their 11-plus exam and went to grammar school, all of which played union. Rugby league-supporting boys like Ray French and Fran Cotton both took this path and eventually ended up playing union for England.

This was not necessarily a natural progression and was often imposed on reluctant adolescents. Boys who played league for a local club outside school were sometimes threatened with exclusion from the school team by union-loving games masters. Occasionally, a school's refusal to play league was often actively opposed by the boys themselves, as the sociologists Brian Jackson and Dennis Marsden explained in their study of working-class education in 1950s Huddersfield:

A recurring situation at Marburton College seems to have been the desire of working-class boys to play rugby league football instead of soccer. When this reached the state of groups of boys organising themselves into something like unofficial school or house teams, then the school might put out feelers for compromise, and suggest the difficulty of catering for rugby union as well as soccer – difficulties say over fixtures of the better kind. The whole point, of course, of the rugby-playing was lost on this, for the school had failed to see that whereas rugby league was very close at heart to northern working-class life, and whereas soccer could occupy a kind of neutral and classless position, rugby union was almost as remote as lacrosse, and not what was wanted at all.

The RFL was well aware of the problems that the game faced at the youth level. Starting in 1958, it gave free playing kit to all U19 teams and in 1961 reorganised youth rugby into U17 and U19 age groups for school-leavers. These reforms went some way to alleviating the situation. A 1964 census reported the number of players aged between 17 and 19 grew by 28 per cent. Under 17s increased by 90 per cent in Lancashire and 38 per cent in Yorkshire. In 1965, the school game was taken over by the newly-formed English Schools Rugby League, which aimed 'to foster the physical, mental, social and moral development of the schoolboys of England in every type of school through the medium of rugby league football'.

But the prejudices of the British educational system meant this was not as straight forward as it might appear. When comprehensive schools were introduced in the 1960s and '70s, many thought their egalitarian ethos would lead to league being played by more schools. In fact, the opposite happened. Many league-playing former secondary modern schools switched from league to union (as the author's 11-year-old self discovered to his horror), so they could play ex-grammar schools that were now comprehensives but had no intention of playing league. It wasn't until the late 1970s, when league's public profile had increased, that it began to regain ground in comprehensive schools, and by 1990 a record 865 schools played rugby league. This was not only due to greater awareness of the game – not least thanks to the amazing Kangaroo touring teams of the 1980s – but also because the expansion of university and college education in the 1960s allowed rugby league-loving schoolboys to become teachers and pass on their passion for the sport to their pupils.

However, the adult amateur game still struggled to keep afloat. By 1965 the number of amateur sides had shrunk to its lowest level since before the First World War. Many blamed the professional clubs, who not only rarely paid amateur clubs when signing one of their players, but also appeared to do little to support the amateur game in their towns. Even more of them blamed the RFL, and especially its secretary Bill Fallowfield, who had little time for amateur rugby league. In 1967 he criticised amateur volunteers who:

> Think they are doing rugby league a favour by either playing rugby league or indulging in the hobby of looking after an amateur team. At other sports, one finds that the attitude is that people are playing the game or organising clubs because they like to do it and are prepared to pay a little for their hobby.

This was not only insulting, but his description of the game as a 'hobby' wilfully ignored the broader community role that the amateur game played. The neglect of amateur rugby league came to a head in in 1973, when amateur officials led by Maurice Oldroyd and Tom Keaveney decided to form an association to promote and safeguard the amateur game. Their move was also in response to the formation of the Sports Council in 1972, which was responsible for providing grants to amateur sports organisations. However, because amateur rugby league was administered by the professional RFL, amateur clubs were not eligible for funding.

So, in May 1973, the British Amateur Rugby League Association (BARLA) was formed at the George Hotel in Huddersfield. Fallowfield immediately ordered professional clubs to stop BARLA teams using their facilities, withdrew RFL support for any amateur side joining the new body and issued a libel writ against the *Hull Daily Mail* for publishing pro-BARLA letters. Fallowfield inadvertently had poked a wasp's nest, and support poured in for the rebels. In May 1974, as Fallowfield's regime ended, the RFL Council saw sense and abandoned the fight, recognising BARLA as the governing body of amateur rugby league.

Freed from a straitjacket, the amateur game blossomed. Barely two years after formation, BARLA had 300 clubs organised in 20 district leagues, and had drawn up a five-year plan not only for the North of England, but also for the South, the Midlands and at all levels of education. Energised by the skills and commitment of Oldroyd, BARLA grew to over 400 clubs in 1985, for the first time in rugby league history, and over 500 by 1990, making it the second largest 'rugby' organisation in the British Isles after the RFU. The following year it was strong enough to establish a national league for the top amateur sides, which expanded to become the four-division National Conference League. Such was the rise in playing standard of the NCL's clubs that giant-killing wins against semi-professional sides in the early rounds of the Challenge Cup no longer became a surprise in the 21st century.

Indeed, BARLA even tried to steal rugby union's thunder by presenting itself as the 'most amateur rugby organisation in the world'.

On its 1978 tour of Australia, New Zealand and Papua New Guinea – the first of its many overseas trips – each player raised their own funds to pay for travel. The only things they received were an official tie, holdall and tracksuit. For BARLA (and rugby league in general) the only definition of 'amateur' was that the player did not get paid, nothing more, nothing less. In contrast to the twelve dense pages of the rugby union's amateur rules, BARLA used just ten words: 'Players shall not receive payment for playing amateur rugby league.' Unlike the RFU, BARLA did not believe amateurism was morally superior to professionalism – it was just the way most people played sport.

Unlike previous generations of league missionaries, the expansion of higher education from the 1960s, and the social and geographical mobility it provided meant BARLA also had a volunteer cadre to take the game beyond the north.

In 1965, a London Amateur Rugby League Association had been founded, and in 1967 students at Leeds University formed the first university rugby league club. By 1980, there were almost two dozen student sides across Britain, often created in the face of institutional opposition from the student rugby union officials.

The number of clubs outside of 'non-traditional' areas also grew, so much so that, by 1990, they represented ten per cent of the 502 amateur clubs. By 1995, almost a quarter of all amateur rugby league clubs came from outside the heartlands or from higher education and, by the time of BARLA's 30th birthday, the game could proudly boast that, for the first time ever, there was an amateur rugby league club in every county in England.

16

•

Evolution of the Rules

'Rugby league is like chess with muscles.'
— Brian Redhead,
BBC Radio 4 *Today* presenter, 1985.

At one minute past midnight on 22 April 1955, Alexander James Murphy signed a contract to become a professional rugby league player with St Helens, his hometown club. It was his 16th birthday, the legal age at which a contract could be signed. He would quickly prove to be the best signing the club ever made. Explosive off the mark and able to pass and kick with precise accuracy and intelligence, he starred as an 18-year-old on the 1958 Lions's tour, playing out of his skin in the second Test at Brisbane when a depleted British side led by Alan Prescott, who played 78 minutes of the match with a broken arm, defeated Australia 25-18 to set up an Ashes series win in the following third encounter. 'Alexander the Great' would not cease to be a star even after he hung up his boots, and went on to be a hugely successful coach.

But Murphy was possessed of something more than

brilliant skills; he also had a razor-sharp football brain. All players would be victims of the rules of the game, but with Murphy, the rules became the victim of the player. It was his incessant kicking to touch to give Saints the scrum head and feed in the 1966 Wembley win over Wigan that led to the touch-kicking rules being changed. It was widely believed that the value of a drop-goal, too, was reduced from two points to one in 1972 because Murphy's Leigh side was so successful using it.

Murphy had a mind that sought every possible advantage, not least in his ability to exploit the tiniest ambiguity or loophole in the rules. 'It's up to any player of recognised top-flight calibre to try and "get away with a little bit of something" out there on the field,' he wrote in his 1967 autobiography, *Saints Hit Double Top*. 'Rules aren't meant to be broken. But it's a challenge to any player worth his salt to try and get away with bending them a little.'

In this, Murphy was the heir to Jonty Parkin. It was an attitude both shared – and it would be one of the decisive factors that would shape the development of the rules of rugby league for over a century.

*****

Rugby's great split was not only about money and class, it was also about how rugby should be played.

Between 1895 and 1906, the Northern Union gradually transformed a game based around scrums and scoring goals into one that emphasised running, passing and scoring tries. But the evolution of the game did not stop with the play-the-ball and thirteen-a-side rugby, as the sport continued to grapple with a key problem for all handling codes of football: what happens once the ball carrier is tackled?

Alex Murphy kicks one of his two drop-goals for Warrington at the 1974 Challenge Cup final

Rugby union's answer, that a ruck, a maul or scrum be formed so that forwards can struggle for possession of the ball, was rejected because it reduced the opportunities for open rugby. American and Canadian football solved the problem by replacing the scrum with the orderly scrimmage and by introducing the concept of 'downs'. The North Americans also dealt with the struggle for possession by simply abolishing it.

In contrast, rugby league sought to regulate the struggle for possession and make it secondary to the running, handling and tackling features of the game. Even so, the problems caused by the scrum and the play-the-ball in the 'struggle for possession' would continue to torment the game throughout the 20th century. Indeed, the very first major gathering of RFL officials after the First World War was a special conference in 1921 to discuss scrums.

165

It was felt there were too many, that they had to be reset too often, and that the ball rarely emerged quickly from them. Hookers – a name for the position which was just coming into common use in preference to the older terms 'striker' or centre-forward – were accused of trying to get an unfair advantage by putting their legs across the tunnel formed by the scrum. Props were also accused of the same offences, while scrum-halves were criticised for their refusal to put the ball into the middle. But rather than change the rules, the conference suggested new 'guidelines' for referees, which did little to alleviate the problem.

In 1930, the rules were changed to force forwards to pack down with three in the front row, two in the second row and a loose forward binding the second row – designed to prevent teams having four in the front row and collapsing the scrum – and in 1932 hookers were forbidden to have a loose arm. These changes usually led to an initial spate of hookers being sent off but then, shortly after, the same problems emerged again. The problem was that scrum-halves and hookers continuously attempted to break the rules to gain an advantage.

Rule-breaking was almost inherent in the very nature of the scrum. When Australian hooker Ken Kearney arrived to play for Leeds in 1948, he asked a referee what the best tactics were to use in English scrums. 'Cheat,' was the one-word reply he allegedly, but quite believably, received.

By the late 1930s, it was not uncommon to see matches with 80 scrums and the failure to find a long-term solution to that problem led to calls for its abolition. In 1938, John Wilson proposed a soccer-style throw-in from touch instead of a scrum, with the caveat that it couldn't be thrown forward. After an experimental game against Bramley in 1947, which used the throw-in, the touring New Zealand team's managers concluded that: 'We must never lose sight of the fact that the scrummage is part of the rugby game and that it would wrong to do away with it and thus lose the advantage of having big strong men in our game.'

The following year, Australian Board of Control secretary Keith Sharp saw Hunslet's 'A' team play Wakefield Trinity 'A' using the throw-in and was even less enthusiastic, arguing it would be used for time-wasting and eventually become identical to the line-out.

In contrast to the British, the Southern Hemisphere authorities believed there was little wrong with the rules, as long as they were properly enforced by referees and adhered to by players.

Although there were long-standing differences in interpretation – for example, the Australian insistence on punishing a forward pass with a penalty for off-side (because the catcher was in front of the passer) rather than a scrum (as in Britain) – was a continual source of friction for almost 70 years. These were not deep-rooted differences. Indeed, Australian and New Zealand players sometimes seemed more inclined to play to the spirit of the law. In 1948, British fans were surprised that the Kangaroo tourists got up quickly from tackles to play the ball, in contrast to the slow ones seen in the English game.

At the same time as the throw-in experiment was taking place, the new RFL secretary Bill Fallowfield proposed experimenting with a rugby union-style method of releasing the ball after the tackle.

Initially, this wasn't taken too seriously because it was one of numerous ideas suggested as a way of stopping teams monopolising possession for long periods. Especially in important matches, teams minimised the risk of losing possession by continuously having the acting half-back pick the ball up from the play-the-ball and run forward without passing, tackle after tackle after tackle. Nicknamed the 'creeping barrage' by *Yorkshire Post* journalist Eric Stanger, one of the most notorious examples happened during the 1951 Championship semi-final at Central Park, when Workington Town, reduced to twelve men due to injury, defended an 8-5 lead against Wigan with 15 minutes left to play. Gus Risman, Town's captain-coach, ordered his players not to pass or kick the ball:

> They would be tackled, play the ball to the acting half-back, who would move forward two yards and then go down in a tackle. He would then play the ball to the acting-half-back, who would move forward two yards and then go down in a tackle. And so it went on ad infinitum.

To solve the problem, Fallowfield and Leigh chairman Jack Hilton proposed using the rugby union method of playing the ball after a tackle at the International Board's October 1954 meeting. The other three nations rejected it out of hand, with French secretary Antoine Blain arguing that, 'to adopt the rugby union method [of playing the ball] would be to step back 50 years, which would be bad'.

Despite its problems, the play-the-ball was regarded by virtually everyone in the game as superior to rugby union's rucking and mauling, and was one of the reasons why French journalists in the 1930s nicknamed the sport 'lightning rugby'. But opposition from the other league nations did little to dampen Fallowfield's enthusiasm for the idea and, at the 1955 Challenge Cup final, he received support from a very unlikely source in the shape of the Duke of Edinburgh, who told Lord Derby, the patron of the RFL, that he didn't like the play-the-ball because it had 'all the disadvantages' of American football.

A royal seal of disapproval was treated by Fallowfield as an endorsement that could not be resisted. A few weeks after the Cup final he called for next season's Lancashire and Yorkshire Cup competitions to use the rugby union rule to play the ball. But Prince Philip's opinions counted for little. Both the Lancashire and Yorkshire committees flatly refused to use the union rule, and the experiment was never tried.

The following year, a questionnaire was circulated to all 30 professional clubs asking their opinions on the play-the-ball, but only three wanted to try the union rule. Two experimental matches were staged in October 1956, but both were described by the press as 'a farce'.

There was widespread opposition to abandoning the play-the-ball throughout the game. Dewsbury's George Oldroyd argued that the problems of the play-the-ball were due to the gamesmanship of professional players, as the problem didn't occur in amateur or schoolboy rugby league.

At a conference of former players and officials called to discuss standards of play in 1954, which included Jim Sullivan, Alec Fiddes and John Wilson (all originally from union backgrounds) no-one mentioned the union rule. Indeed, outside of Fallowfield and one or two club directors, nobody else spoke in favour of it. This was not surprising. The first principle of playing rugby league was to keep hold of the ball. The greatest crime was to lose it. Players who had spent their entire sporting lives adhering to these principles would not easily or willingly abandon this truth.

This did not deter Fallowfield. In 1961, he arranged an experimental match between British and French sides in Paris using players chosen for their familiarity with rugby union.

Ray French, who won four England union caps before

joining St Helens, recalled, '...the game was a disaster and many of us spent the whole evening scratching and scrambling on the floor for the ball.' Fallowfield raised the issue again in November 1963. He argued the rugby union method of releasing the ball in the tackle had 'stood the test of time' and that the play-the-ball, 'reduces the chances of the rugby league game appealing to a much wider public'. He therefore organised a new competition to test his ideas, the 'Bottom Fourteen Play-Offs' for those clubs finishing in the wrong half of the league table. Each team had one tackle with a standard rugby league play-the-ball, but on the second tackle they had to release the ball rugby union-style.

To say the tournament was unpopular would be giving it too much praise. Four clubs refused to take part and those that did demanded the RFL subsidise their matches because of poor attendances. Its last shred of credibility was destroyed three weeks before the opening matches when an emergency meeting of the clubs voted against any rule changes. The tournament was now to be played under a rule that would never be implemented. Yet again, rugby league seemed to be a sport whose administrators could not make up their minds about its future. David Watkins, the Wales rugby union captain who signed for Salford in 1967 for a record-breaking £15,000, remembered that in his first years in the game, 'there were confusions and anomalies under the Fallowfield regime which made Rugby League football hard for spectators to follow and, let me add, for players to play!'

Why was such a state of affairs allowed to happen?

The severe financial problems facing the game from the late 1950s led to a great deal of disorientation among its leadership. Fallowfield filled the vacuum with a vision of rugby league that was essentially professional thirteen-a-side rugby union.

In 1963, he wrote to RFU secretary Robin Prescott about the play-the-ball rule saying 'I can never see why it was instituted in the first place.' As well as wanting to adopt the rugby union play-the-ball rule he was also an early enthusiast of the throw-in from touch proposal.

The lack of direction or strategy for the game meant that rugby union ideas could become influential. Although Fallowfield was born into a rugby league family in Barrow, he went to Cambridge University before the war and made two appearances as a wing-forward for England in war-time internationals. He even played for Moortown RUFC until the early 1950s, despite his position as RFL secretary. His views reflected a frustration on the part of some club directors that rugby league was not able to escape from its working-class roots. 'It is difficult for [rugby league supporters and officials] to look at the game objectively. Their interest is primarily in winning rather than being entertained,' he argued in 1966.

The irony of Fallowfield's position was that it was rugby union which was taking rules from rugby league. In 1948, the RFU had reduced the drop-goal from four to three points. In 1970, kicking the ball directly into touch had been only allowed from behind the kicking side's 25 yard line, a variation on league's 'ball back' rule. The following year, the value of a try was increased to four points, the first time in union's history that a try was worth more than a goal, and was raised again in 1992 to five points.

From the late 1980s, as the pressure to professionalise rugby union continued to rise, there were numerous rule changes to speed up the ball's release after a tackle, causing several commentators to observe that the new laws were making union appear more like league. In fact, union was beginning its journey down the same evolutionary road that league had been travelling on since 1895.

A new stage in that evolution came at the July 1966 meeting of the Rugby League International Board, when the debate about the play-the-ball was surprisingly settled once and for all.

The British, represented by Fallowfield and Hull KR director Wilf Spaven, once again put the play-the-ball on the agenda. As usual, the other three nations were opposed to any change. But the Australians were now also seeking a solution to a domestic problem. St George had won the Sydney premiership ten consecutive times, and would add to it once more later that year. The Dragons' complete domination meant the Australians were now more open to ideas to make the game more competitive. On the first day of the meeting Fallowfield referred to American football and its rule which dictated a transfer of possession after four downs, and proposed that a team should have three play-the-balls, following which a scrum should be formed if tackled in possession on the fourth tackle. For the first time in two decades, all four countries agreed and voted to try the new four-tackle rule.

In England, the new rule was trialled in the BBC2 Floodlit Trophy competition in October 1966, and it soon became clear that it encouraged attacking play. Less than a month later, the RFL decided the four-tackle rule could be used in league matches if both teams agreed. This meant clubs could decide to play different rules against different opponents. So Leeds chose to play the four tackle rule against a weak Doncaster side, but the unlimited tackle rule against the Challenge Cup holders St Helens, much to the annoyance of the latter. Caught in a mess caused by their own enthusiasm, the RFL announced that from October 31, all matches would be played under the four tackle rule, giving clubs one week to prepare.

Fortunately, the success of the rule overcame the confusion of its introduction, and Norman Gaulton wrote in the *Rugby League Magazine* that: 'Skill and enterprise have been given far more rein during these last few months, and the variety of tactics and the spirit of adventure which have been so sadly lacking has been reintroduced again.'

From Australia, Bill Buckley told the RFL the new rule had 'revitalised' the game down under. The new rule also helped end St George's amazing premiership run when they were finally defeated by Canterbury-Bankstown in the 1967 preliminary final. For teams like St George, who built their game on incessant forward drives to give their backs a platform for attack, or who lacked a strong tactical kicker, the new rule created tremendous difficulties. Four tackles often led to team's panicking and passing the ball wildly, so in 1972 the rule was extended to six tackles following two trials in Sydney, marking a further move away from union's contest for possession.

Over the next ten years, rugby league continued to move further away from its rugby union past.

In 1974, the drop-goal was reduced from two points to one. In 1983, a handover of the ball to the opposing side, rather than a scrum, was introduced when the attacking side was tackled with the ball on the sixth tackle. The value of a try was also raised to four points in 1983, emphasising that the essence of the game was to score tries. The historic struggle to reform the scrum was abandoned in the 1990s by informally allowing the ball to be fed directly to the scrum-half's own forwards. Striking for the ball at the play-the-ball, or playing it to oneself, was also outlawed in the opening season of Super League in 1996 and in 2020, as discussions were held by the RFL as to how the game should safely emerge from lockdown during the coronavirus crisis, the proposal was made to at least temporarily ditch the scrum altogether.

These rule changes removed the last traces of the struggle for the ball with the feet, and consolidated the game as primarily one about territory. In 1993, the importance of territory was cemented with the introduction of the rule that forced the defending side to stand ten metres back from the play-the-ball. This had always been a shifting border, with sides initially not having to retreat at all but then being forced backwards to three yards and then five. The change to ten metres shifted the dynamics, placing a premium on running forwards and increasing the importance of repeated sets of play-the-balls to create pressure through momentum.

Sport, no less than the natural world, is governed by evolution and rugby league's rules have evolved by responding to the challenges inherent in all handling codes of football. The problems of possession, the tackle and the scrum had been solved by pragmatic changes to the rules, which were based on the common understanding that rugby was a game of running, passing, tackling and try-scoring, and that it should be, in the words of Hull chairman Charles Simpson in 1903, a 'game without monotony.'

17
•
Anglo-Australian Relations:
The Intangible Bond

'To east coast Australians, Yorkshire and Lancashire
towns are more relevant to their education than the
Tower of London ... in the North, to be Australian was
to be welcomed, to be an Australian on the rugby league
trail ensured a hospitality bred of an intangible bond.'
– Adrian MacGregor, journalist, 1990.

Malcolm Reilly was just 22 when he arrived in Australia on
the 1970 Lions' tour. Strong and fast with an incisive handling
and kicking game, he combined a supreme footballing brain
with a ferocious commitment to winning.

A week before the first Test, he was at a party where he
was continuously taunted as a 'Pommie bastard'. Provoked
beyond endurance he punched the perpetrator, who called
the police. The police took no action, but the incident quickly
made the front pages of the Australian tabloids. In a society
where rugby league dominated the media, Reilly became
public enemy number one in the press.

He had has revenge. With the series tied one-all and less than two minutes remaining, the Lions were hanging on to an 18-17 lead. Then Reilly slipped out a slide-rule pass to put Doug Laughton away. He found the supporting Roger Millward, who raced 40 yards to claim the Ashes-winning try. Commentating on television, Eddie Waring's voice cracked with joy as Millward raced away to score: 'Millward, Millward, Millwaaaard...' he shouted, as the little maestro touched down. It was one of the great Ashes series, but it was also the last time Britain would win them for at least 50 years.

The following year, 1971, Reilly returned down under when he moved from Castleford to Manly for a then world record £15,000 fee. He repaid the Sea Eagles every penny, playing a pivotal role in their 1972 and '73 Grand Final wins. He then returned down under in 1995 to coach the Newcastle Knights to their first-ever premiership. Loved by fans, feared by opponents and celebrated equally in both Britain and Australia, Malcolm Reilly was the embodiment of the intangible bond that united league across the hemispheres.

He would also prove to be something of a prophet.

When he came home to Castleford in 1975, he told the *John Player Rugby League Yearbook* that Australians, '...take the game more seriously ... They go for superb fitness and it shows in their game, which is very physical. If ever the Aussies do match us for tactics, then with their superior fitness they will be unbeatable.'

*****

The passion generated by the 1970 Ashes series demonstrated the crucial importance to British rugby league of its links with Australia. Locked as it was into the geographical confines of three counties in the north of England, the spread of the game to Australia and New Zealand in 1907 was crucial to the consolidation of rugby league's distinct identity. As the *Athletic News* pointed out in 1923, '...one phase of the game attracts interest even outside Lancashire and Yorkshire ... the periodical visits of British teams to Australasia and Australasian teams to England.'

Despite Albert Baskerville's Kiwi tourists pioneering international rugby league in 1907, the British always viewed Australia as the main enemy.

New Zealand rugby league struggled to compete with the union juggernaut at home, and the game there remained an amateur sport until the 1980s. This financial weakness meant that early Kangaroo teams which toured Britain were technically joint sides – the 1911 tour included four Kiwis but only one in 1921. It was not until 1926 that another independent Kiwi tour to Britain was organised, which proved to be a disaster on and off the field, and that was followed by the trip in 1939, quickly truncated after World War Two broke out after the first game. It was only in 1947 that Kiwi tours resumed and became a regular part of the league calendar.

In contrast, Anglo-Australian Test matches were regarded as the pinnacle of the sport even before World War One. In 1920, Australia regained the Ashes, but the following year the symbolic trophy was snatched back in a thrilling series. A solitary Jim Sullivan conversion ten minutes from time in the second Test of 1924 kept the Ashes in Britain and the 1928 series was a similarly tight affair.

In 1929-30, both sides won a match and drew the third Test 0-0 at Swinton after Australia's Chimpy Busch had a last-minute try controversially disallowed, so an unprecedented fourth Test was hastily arranged to decide the series. Harry Waller, the first chairman of the Northern Union in 1895, was so outraged he protested to the RFL that 'Mammon has won,' and that the Ashes would be 'worthless' if an extra Test was played. But almost 17,000 spectators proved the Ashes were far from that, when they packed into Rochdale's Athletic Grounds on a Wednesday afternoon to see an impossibly tight match won on 73 minutes by a solitary unconverted try from Leeds winger Stan Smith. Once again, as they would do for the next 20 years, the Ashes stayed in England.

The drawn third Test at Swinton in 1930 was also noteworthy, for its brutality. 'To call it a game is a misnomer,' wrote the *Yorkshire Post*. 'War is a more appropriate term.'

The 1932 tour to Australia became notorious for its second Test, the so-called 'Battle of Brisbane', won by Australia despite being reduced to ten men at one point due to injuries. In 1936, Australian forward Ray Stehr achieved the unprecedented feat of being sent off twice in the same Test series. Clive Churchill's lasting memory of the 1948 Kangaroo tour was the violence they faced from English club sides. Perhaps the depths were finally plumbed in the 1954 Britain versus New South Wales tour match, which was abandoned by the referee after just 16 minutes of the second half due to uncontrollable fighting. The 1960s saw more players sent off for violence in Test matches than in any other decade, culminating in the 1970 World Cup final 'Battle of Leeds' at Headingley, when brawling continued well after the final whistle, leading to outrage in the daily newspapers.

But despite the high profile of league in Australia, such violence never led to calls to break off relations between the two countries. Australian rugby league officials were fundamentally loyal to the British Empire until the 1960s. 'We are just as British as you are,' protested Harry 'Jersey' Flegg, the president of the New South Wales Rugby League in 1950, during a dispute with British tour manager George Oldroyd.

'Australians look to England as the mother country in war, in industry and also in rugby league football,' Queensland selector E. S. Brown told the RFL Council in 1954, because, 'there is a strong desire in Australia to get along with England from every point of view'.

For Australians, rugby league combined loyalty to the British Empire and, contradictorily, hostility to privilege. Lions' tours were captained by workers from the industrial heartlands of Britain – almost uniquely among British travellers of the time – and the players were working men, just like Australian players and spectators. Touring British sides resembled Australia more than they did Britain: ostensibly working-class, democratic and meritocratic. The most memorable example of this attitude was seen before a match in Sydney, when Jersey Flegg was introduced to a visiting British dignitary, Lord MacDonald. Flegg misheard his name and greeted him with 'G'day Claude.' When Australian Governor-General Bill McKell told him: 'No Jerse, it's Lord, not Claude,' Flegg replied. 'We don't go with that bullshit here. This is Australia.'

The importance of the bond between British and Australian league was highlighted in 1945, when the RFL Council met with the Australian Minister of External Affairs, Dr Herbert Evatt. A high court judge at the age of 36, a future leader of the Australian Labour Party and shortly to become the first president of the UN's General Assembly, Evatt was also a dyed-in-the-wool rugby league supporter who set up Sydney University's rugby league team when a student there.

While en route to America, he made a special trip to Manchester to persuade the RFL to send a touring team to Australia. The war had barely ended and the RFL thought it would be too difficult to organise a tour. 'The close relationships that have been built up between Australia and

Official Souvenir Programme

THE QUEENSLAND RUGBY LEAGUE

GUS RISMAN, England's Captain

GAZETTE

England v. Queensland
Played at the Brisbane Cricket Ground, Brisbane
SATURDAY, JUNE 22, 1946
PRICE 6d.

A programme from June 1946, Lions captain Gus Risman on the cover

New Zealand and the North of England is in the nature of a history and the building up of this history ought to be resumed as soon as possible, in the best interests of rugby league football and of the Empire,' he told the meeting. The RFL agreed and, thanks to help from the Australian government, the Lions departed in April 1946, aboard the Royal Navy aircraft carrier, *HMS Indomitable*.

Travelling to Australia was not the only problem the 1946 Lions faced. The RFL issued each player with a trunk to carry their belongings down under with them, but most players had trouble filling it. Although the war had ended, rationing was still in operation and clothing of any type could only be bought if one had the right coupons. 'I have found it difficult to obtain sufficient clothing for the trip,' tour captain Gus Risman told the *Daily Despatch*. 'I shall travel in my demob suit [the suit issued to soldiers when they left the army]. My football boots have been patched so often that there are now more patches than the original leather on the uppers.'

His wife, Ethel, said: 'It has been an awful job. I have patched and darned so that Gus could save his coupons for the tour, but we have barely managed to scrape through.' When the tourists arrived in Australia they were showered with gifts, including food parcels to send home to their families. One of Risman's duties as captain when the Lions' visited New South Wales and Queensland country towns was to receive a symbolic food parcel of local products as part of Australia's support for what they still saw as the 'Mother Country'.

This close relationship between Britain and Australia did not mean there were no disputes between officials. The RFL jealously guarded its status as the game's ultimate decision-making body, voting down a proposal in 1927 to establish an Imperial Rugby League Board. The only advice it seems to have taken from the Australians was to change its name from the Northern Union to the Rugby Football League in 1922. It was only in 1948 that the RFL supported the creation of an International Board (IB), but even then insisted that the RFL secretary would be the IB secretary and the RFL would decide on any rule changes. The Australians only joined late in 1949, when it was agreed that all IB decisions had to be unanimous.

The relationship came under serious pressure in the 1960s, as the political relationship between the two nations changed.

In 1961, Harold Macmillan's government announced Britain would join the European Common Market without consulting Australia, and ended free entry into Britain for all

Commonwealth citizens, including those from Australia. The 1960s also saw Australians questioning their previous deferential attitudes towards Britain, and in rugby league this meant that the British game was no longer regarded as being inherently superior.

The major source of international antagonism had historically been the poaching of antipodean players by wealthy English clubs. Six of the first New Zealand tourists and ten of the first Kangaroos joined English sides, some of them, such as Wigan's Lance Todd and Huddersfield's Albert Rosenfeld, becoming household names and adding an international glamour unique in British sport at that time. But the Australians protested at the loss of their best players, and in November 1909 were given a veto over signings and transfers dried up.

However, in June 1927, the British clubs forced the transfer ban to be lifted, opening the gates for a wave of exciting players. The likes of Ernest Mills and Ray Markham at Huddersfield, Vic Hey, Eric Harris and Jeff Moores at Leeds, Hector Gee at Wigan and Bill Shankland at Warrington were among many who lit up British rugby league from the late 1920s. By the mid-1930s the player drain had reached such levels that journalists wondered if Australia would ever again win a Test series against the British. The problem could have been solved by the simple expediency of allowing players with English clubs to play for the Kangaroos, but exiled players were not eligible for international selection. In 1911, Warrington's Dan Frawley, a 1908 Kangaroo, wanted to play for touring Australians, but the Northern Union ruled that a player's responsibility was to his club alone.

The performance of the 1937 Kangaroos was so poor that the RFL agreed to an international transfer ban. It lapsed during the war, and when peace came British clubs resumed signing players from the Antipodes. The ban was re-imposed in 1947, but not before many clubs had picked off many of Australia's top players. Those signed in 1946 and 1947 made an indelible mark on the British game, among them Brian Bevan, Harry Bath, Arthur Clues, Lionel Cooper, Pat Devery, and Johnny Hunter. Bevan became the most prolific try-scorer ever, with 740 touchdowns for Warrington in 620 games. Hunter, Devery and Cooper were the crucial triumvirate in Huddersfield's success of the early 1950s. Arthur Clues and a complete three-quarter line of fellow Australians brought glamour, if not glory, to Headingley.

British clubs then realised the 1947 ban did not apply to rugby union players, so Rochdale Hornets decided to persuade Australian league players to switch temporarily to rugby union, making them free to move to England. In 1950, Hornets signed five junior rugby league players using this subterfuge, until the Australian Board of Control persuaded the RFL to outlaw it. British scouts turned to established Australian union players, such as Wallaby captain Trevor Allen and future league TV commentator Rex Mossop, both of whom signed for Leigh. In 1951, the furious Australian authorities forced the RFL to agree that all signings, whether from league or union, had to be agreed by the player's domestic rugby league authorities.

The success of Australian players in the post-war years highlighted how much the two countries had in common. The vast majority of imported players quickly became part of their local communities and slipped easily into the local culture. Albert Rosenfeld lived in Huddersfield until he died in 1970, working for most of his life as a dustman. Arthur Clues, famous for his ferocious assaults on the 1946 British Lions, settled in Leeds and became one of its most prominent sporting celebrities and charity fund-raisers. Rex Mossop's comments about Leigh in the 1950s seem to echo the feelings of many players: 'I loved these loyal supporters, the way they'd cheer and sing at matches and shout you a pint in their cosy, friendly pubs. They made you feel part of a community.'

The ban on international transfers had the desired effect and Australia finally regained the Ashes in 1950, on a muddy Sydney Cricket Ground, when winger Ron Roberts dived over in the corner 15 minutes from time for a series-winning 5-2 victory. Britain retook the crown in 1952, faltered again in 1954, but then held the Ashes from 1956. However, in 1963 Australia shocked even themselves and took the series by winning the first two matches, 28-2 and 50-12. The second Test at Swinton was the first time either side had scored a half-century of points in an Ashes match – and was a portent of what was to come.

One reason for the reversal of British fortunes in the 1960s was that Australia now had a large number of players who went home after honing their skills in England. When future Australia coach Harry Bath returned from Warrington to play for St George in 1957, he was shocked: 'I couldn't believe the bash and barge way Saints played the game. Blokes knocking themselves stupid. I thought "Christ! This isn't for me".' Dick Huddart, the British second-row forward who moved to St George in the 1960s, credited Bath with revolutionising Australian forward play: '...before Harry showed them how to play, Australian forwards were called pigs, and that's how they played ... all they'd do was put their heads down, get tackled and die with the ball.' Much of the success of St George's record eleven consecutive premierships was due to the British techniques learned by Bath and captain-coach Ken Kearney, a Leeds player from 1948 to 1952.

It also helped that, in the 1950s, Australian rugby league was undergoing a financial revolution. In 1956, poker

Above: Children in 1963 bought this comic, *The Hornet*, with Neil Fox on the cover

RICHARD HARRIS
"THIS SPORTING LIFE"
RACHEL ROBERTS
Alan BADEL
William HARTNELL

SCREENPLAY BY / PRODUCED BY / DIRECTED BY
DAVID STOREY / KAREL REISZ / LINSAY ANDERSON
A JULIAN WINTLE-LESLIE PARKYN PRODUCTION
FOR THE RANK ORGANIZATION
A WALTER READE-STERLING PRESENTATION

INTERNATIONAL FILM CRITICS' PRIZE
'BEST ACTOR OF THE YEAR' AWARD
1963 CANNES
FILM FESTIVAL

Above: The 1963 film adaptation of David Storey's novel of 1960, *This Sporting Life*, took rugby league into cinemas but divided opinion among the game's supporters

Above: Willie Horne shows off the Lancashire County Cup after captaining Barrow to a 12–2 victory over Oldham at Station Road, Swinton, in 1954

Left: The best – and cockiest – scrum-half in the business, Alex Murphy

Right: Balmain win the Wills Cup in 1976 down under, led by Brian Lockwood

Above: The cover of the Challenge Cup programme in 1980 for the all-Hull final

Left: Malcolm Reilly, from the coal town of Castleford, in action against Australia in 1970

A MAN'S GAME

2/6

10 YEARS IN ENGLISH
RUGBY LEAGUE by *Vic Hey*

Left: Vic Hey's book, *A Man's Game*, and Gus Risman's *Rugby Renegade*, below, were two of the first RL autobiographies

GUS RISMAN
From Rugby Union honours to the best known personality in Rugby League football

Rugby Renegade

Below: Hull legend Clive Sullivan collects the World Cup in 1972 – the most recent time Great Britain have won the tournament

Above: Lucius Banks, the American footballer who was at Hunslet in 1912

Left: Cec Thompson, the second black player to represent Great Britain

Below: Johnny Freeman and Barry Robinson celebrate Halifax's 15-7 victory over St. Helens in the 1964-65 Championship final at Station Road, Swinton

Left: Ellery Hanley receives a Greatest Ever Great Britain Player award at Huddersfield's then-Galpharm Stadium, before a GB v New Zealand Test match in 2007

Above: Hull FC's wheelchair team in training at the Bonus Youth Performance Centre in 2019. The wheelchair variant is a modern-day success story   *SWpix.com*

Above: Elisabeth Beal, pioneering girl RL player; programmes from 2000 and 2002

Above: Coral Women's Challenge Cup Final – University of Bolton Stadium, 2019.
Leeds captain Courtney Hill dives over for a try against Castleford Tigers   *SWpix.com*

Above and below: England's Sam Burgess leads by example and scores a try during a thrilling World Cup semi-final defeat to New Zealand at Wembley in 2013   *SWpix.com*

machines ('one-armed bandits' in Britain) were legalised in New South Wales and brought in huge amounts of money for clubs. Three years later, the abolition of the residential qualification for players meant they no longer had to live in the immediate catchment area of their club. Sydney rugby league clubs could now match the financial benefits of playing in England.

As the game in Sydney grew richer and ever more popular in the 1960s, the lure of Australia became irresistible for British players. This was also the era of the 'Ten Pound Poms', a scheme which meant anyone could emigrate to Australia from Britain for just £10. In 1960, Phil Jackson, the Barrow centre who starred on the 1958 British tour of Australia, became captain-coach of the Goulburn Workers club, the first British player since Huddersfield forward Ben Gronow became coach of Grenfell in New South Wales in 1925.

In March 1963, Derek Hallas became the first British player in the Sydney Premiership, when he went from Keighley to Parramatta. He was followed by internationals such as Huddart, Dave Bolton, Cliff Watson, Alan Burwell and Tommy Bishop. Ironically, Britain's 1970 Ashes series victory accelerated the exodus, as Australian clubs clamoured to sign the triumphant British stars. The following year, Manly captured Malcolm Reilly, followed by Hull KR's Phil Lowe, who built on Huddart's legacy as a free-running second-row forward. 'As the aircraft carrier made the battleship obsolete, Phil Lowe established that the lumbering forward was about to join the mastodons in extinction,' wrote the Booker Prize-winning author and Manly fanatic Thomas Keneally.

Just as the Australian national side was weakened by a player exodus in the 1930s, now it was the turn of Great

Britain. The 1977 World Cup, in which the British were forced to field an essentially second-string side due to the number of their top players signed to Sydney clubs, led to the RFL forcing a new international transfer ban. Yet it did nothing to close the growing chasm between the two nations, and things went from bad to worse. Between 1979 and 1988, Great Britain did not win a single Test match against Australia. Indeed, they found it extremely difficult even to score – in the 1982 Ashes series they managed a single try in three encounters.

The rise in the Australians' skill, athleticism and tactical awareness was matched only by the British decline. Some of this change was due to the introduction of limited tackle football in the 1960s. Britain's traditional success had been built on continuous forward domination, with ball-playing forwards releasing the ball out of the tackle. But such dominance was impossible to build when the ball could only be held for six tackles. The emphasis of the game switched to fitness and speed, qualities which the Australian game had always possessed. It wasn't until a new generation of British players emerged in the mid-1980s – such as Ellery Hanley, Martin Offiah, Andy Gregory and Garry Schofield – that the gap narrowed, but even they could not win back the Ashes.

Australian coaches were less insular than their British cousins and willing to learn from other sports and other countries. Many of the innovations brought to the game in the 1960s and '70s by coaches like Jack Gibson and Terry Fearnley were taken from American football. Yet the British game suffered from the parochialism and unwillingness to learn common to all British sports. Fitness levels and even basic skills in England lagged far behind those in the southern hemisphere. Many Australian players who played for British clubs in the 1980s were shocked by the poor tackling techniques and defensive know-how of their team-mates.

The larger structural problem for Britain was that for every British player of international standard, the Australians had ten. Unlike the north of England, rugby league dominated the sporting life of Australia's eastern seaboard. This gave it a huge pool of players, significant wealth due to its leagues' clubs and, because of incessant media interest, an intensity of competition which accustomed players to playing in high-pressure matches.

In contrast, British rugby league suffered from what could be called the 'Ryan Giggs problem'. In 1960, the Football League abolished its maximum wage policy. In the past, soccer's restrictions on wages and lack of signing-on fees could make rugby league financially more attractive to young players talented at both games. The relative balance between the two codes can be seen by the fact that future Liverpool and England great Roger Hunt earned just £22 per week in 1960, while Ray French was paid £18 when he made his debut for St Helens the following year.

But from the mid-1960s, the money available in soccer meant young players of both sports almost inevitably opted for the round-ball game.

Michael Appleton played both sports growing up in Manchester, in the 1980s and 1990s: 'As a kid, I had offers in rugby league and football, but I couldn't turn down Manchester United. I was getting better at rugby league and as a 16-year-old I had a decision to make. As soon as United came in, that was it'.

The best example of this was Ryan Giggs, whose father, Danny Wilson, played for Swinton and who himself was sufficiently talented to play rugby league for Lancashire schoolboys. In earlier times, Giggs may well have followed family tradition, but his soccer skills brought him a lucrative professional contract as a teenager and he was lost to league.

The quest to close the gap with Australia dominated the British game from the 1980s. Successive 3-0 Ashes losses in 1984 and 1986 were followed by tighter series over the next decade, yet the gulf remained. Although overseas players were eventually restricted to three per club, few British teams did without them. However, even more influential in the 1980s were Australian coaches such as John Monie at Wigan, Chris Anderson with Halifax and Brian Smith at Hull and Bradford, instrumental in bringing change to the British game and establishing a new tradition of overseas influence on it. Brian Smith's two years at Bradford in the mid-1990s created a whole generation of British coaches, led by Brian Noble, who had learned their craft under him.

Despite almost continuous defeats of the national side, the brilliance of the 1982 and 1986 Kangaroo teams was for many British rugby league supporters a new affirmation of the sport's self-belief and, by the late 1980s, it was a mark of an enlightened rugby league fan to wear an Australian replica club shirt to matches. For them and many others, the Australians were demonstrating that rugby league was indeed the greatest game of all.

Yet by the mid-1990s, events would arise to show how Australians not only dominated the game on the pitch, they now also dictated the course of the game off it.

18

•

Crossing the Colour Line

*'It was bad enough being black... How much lower
down the social scale could one go than be seen as a
black, uneducated rugby league player?'*
– Cec Thompson, Hunslet & Great Britain, 1995.

Growing up in Cardiff in the 1950s, Clive Sullivan's ambition
to become a star rugby player was hampered by two issues.
As a teenager, he was in and out of hospital undergoing
operations on his legs and arms, causing doctors to think he
would never become an athlete. And even without this
disadvantage, his chances of playing for Wales at rugby
union were zero. It was an open secret that no black player
would ever be selected for Wales's national team. Clive had
to look elsewhere to fulfil his ambitions.

At first he tried Bradford Northern, but they showed
little interest so he joined the army. While stationed at
Catterick, in North Yorkshire, he played in a trial match for
Hull and scored a hat-trick. He would become one of the
greatest players in club history, posting 250 tries for them.

When he discovered in 1974 that he no longer figured in Hull's plans, he then moved east to join Hull KR, where he stayed for seven years and scored another 118 tries. He became such an icon in his adopted home city that the main arterial road into Hull was renamed Clive Sullivan Way.

These weren't his only achievements. In 1972, 'Sully' was appointed captain of the Great Britain rugby league team, and later that year he not only scored an unforgettable length-of-the-field try but also became the last British player to hold the World Cup aloft. But Clive was not only the first black player to captain Great Britain, he was also the first black athlete in any game to skipper a British national side. He had achieved his boyhood dream, while also becoming a pioneer for the whole of British sport.

*****

Less than a month after the historic meeting at the George Hotel in 1895, a supporter of the Northern Union wrote to the *Yorkshire Post*: 'I say with Mark Twain's bold, bad boy, that we glory in the sentence of outlawry pronounced on us, as freeing us from the tyrannical bondage of the English Union'.

The 'bold, bad boy' was Huckleberry Finn, who in Twain's famous novel declared he would go to hell rather than betray his friend Jim, a runaway slave. The idea that rugby league was an outlaw sport of the disadvantaged and oppressed would run deep throughout its history.

The first minority group to get involved in the game were the Jewish communities of Hull, Leeds and Manchester. From the early 1890s, Jewish spectators had been prominent at rugby matches in the north, so much so that the Leeds Parish Church side became known as 'the Jewish team,' because of its support from thousands of Jewish immigrants who had settled in the city. There were also local Jewish players, such as Hunslet's Eli Jacobson and Broughton Rangers' Reuben Glaskie. The two most famous Welsh players to 'go north' in the 1890s, brothers David and Evan James, were of Jewish origin and played for Broughton Rangers, a club at the heart of Manchester's Jewish community. Jacobson was a local butcher in Leeds who played twelve times for Yorkshire at rugby union in the mid-1890s, before becoming a stalwart of local amateur rugby league. From 1929, dozens of factory teams in Hunslet competed for the Eli Jacobson Cup named in his honour. And, of course, the most prominent Jewish rugby league player before 1914 was Huddersfield's immortal try-scoring winger Albert Rosenfeld, the son of a Sydney tailor.

The 1920s and 1930s saw Jewish players follow in his footsteps, such as Hull KR's Louis Harris, Rochdale's Sam Birkinshaw and a number of Broughton Rangers' players. Rangers' Lester Samuels, one of the few medical doctors to play rugby league, turned out as an amateur because that allowed him to play on Saturday, the Jewish Sabbath – playing for money would make it work and was therefore forbidden. Broughton had significant Jewish representation among club directors and officials. Barney Manson, born into the Manchester Jewish community but a director of Swinton, became a manager of the 1958 Great Britain touring team. The popularity of league among Jews in Leeds was bemoaned by a number of the more orthodox, most notably mathematician and Zionist leader Selig Brodetsky, who lived in Leeds and complained about the number of Jews he saw going to Headingley on the Sabbath. Reputedly, Yiddish songs were sung on the terraces at Leeds during the 1930s.

The game reflected the society around it and was unfortunately not free of anti-Semitism. 'But we don't bring supporters from Jerusalem,' was the alleged response of a St Helens supporter in 1929, when Salford fans criticised the number of New Zealanders in the Saints' team, and anti-Semitic comments against Leeds could occasionally be heard at matches. The number of Jewish players was never large, but was still more than the four identified by the *Jewish Chronicle* in 1935 who had played in the Football League. Nevertheless, these Jewish rugby league players were an indication of the sport's willingness to recruit on the basis of ability rather than social status or racial origin.

The game's emphasis on merit was highlighted by the emergence of black players. The first black athlete to play professional rugby league seems to have been Lucius Banks, who signed for Hunslet in 1912. Banks, a US soldier, was spotted playing American football by a club official who was in New York on business. The club bought him out of the US Army and over to England, but the strength of Hunslet's back division limited his opportunities and he returned home at the end of the year.

In 1913, Barrow signed James Peters, a dockworker from Plymouth, whose five England caps between 1906 and 1908 made him the sole black player to represent England at rugby union until 1988. Peters signed just as his career was winding down and, despite a move to St Helens, his career effectively ended with the outbreak of World War One. It is impossible to know how many black players played the game at an amateur level, although an anonymous black player is in the team photograph of Pendlebury Northern Union club's Lancashire Junior Cup-winning side of 1903.

During the inter-war years black players made their presence felt as professionals. In 1935, Wigan stand-off George Bennett made the first of three appearances for Wales in their first-ever match against France. Oldham loose-forward Alec Givvons missed only two of Wales's eight matches between 1936 and 1939. In 1937, Broughton's Jimmy Cumberbatch became the first black player to be selected for England, when he scored two tries against France at Thrum Hall. His brother, Val, played for Barrow and scored a try on his debut for England against France in Paris in 1938. The Cumberbatch brothers played for England fully 40 years before Viv Anderson became the first black player to play soccer for England, and this was at a time when the 'colour bar' prevented black boxers from fighting for British championship belts.

The most outstanding black player to emerge in the 1930s was, like Bennett and Givvons, born in Wales. Roy Francis signed for Wigan as a 17-year-old in 1936, but was transferred to Barrow after just twelve matches by the club's new manager Harry Sunderland because, Francis believed, of the colour of his skin. After an outstanding war-time career, in which he starred for Dewsbury at league and, bizarrely, England at union, in 1947 he became the first black player to play for Great Britain. In 1949, he moved to Hull, where he became probably the first black person to coach a professional sports team in Britain. He turned a mediocre side into Championship winners, took them to Wembley twice, and brought to the game motivational techniques, scientific fitness regimes and tactical innovation. He then moved to coach Leeds in 1963, and created one of the club's greatest teams.

The 1950s saw black players become household names in the game. Leeds-born Cec Thompson played for Great Britain in 1951, and in 1960 was appointed as coach of the Barrow club. In 1953, Wigan signed winger Billy Boston, who was such a phenomenon that he was selected for the 1954 GB tour of Australia after just six Wigan matches, becoming the then youngest-ever tourist. Aboriginal Australian player

Wally McArthur, a sprinter frustrated by his treatment at the hands of Australian athletics administrators, returned to his first love of rugby league when he signed for Rochdale in 1953. The following year, Johnny Freeman left Wales to make a career – and a life – in Halifax, where he became arguably the club's best-ever winger.

Both Boston and Freeman came from Cardiff's Tiger Bay docklands' district. The area had been home to African sailors since the 19th century and had one of the largest multiracial populations in Britain before World War Two. Sport was important to the community – the British heavyweight boxing champion of the mid-1950s Joe Erskine was born there – and rugby was especially popular. However, it was an open secret in Wales that no black player would be picked for the Welsh rugby union team. Many black players realised early in their careers they would have to go north if they wanted to play at the highest levels.

In 1961, a young Clive Sullivan was inspired by Boston's success to seek out a rugby league team. Colin Dixon, Frank Wilson, Terry Michael and many others followed in his footsteps. And the fact that these players were warmly welcomed by northern communities – Boston has a statue in Wigan – contrasted sharply with their treatment in Wales.

It wasn't only from Wales that black players came. A number of black rugby union players left apartheid South Africa to play with English league sides in the 1960s and '70s. South African 'coloured' representative player Dave Barends moved to Wakefield Trinity in 1970 and, after he had transferred to Bradford, became the first non-British player to play for Great Britain when selected for the 1979 tour of Australasia – two years before a black player was selected for the Springbok union team. Barends was preceded by other great non-white South Africans, such as Louie Neumann at

Leeds and Ghulam Abed Hussain at Bradford, and would be followed by Green Vigo at Wigan.

The importance of black players in rugby league grew throughout the 1980s and 1990s. Northern English players such as Des Drummond, Henderson Gill, Roy Powell, Martin Offiah, Carl Gibson and Jason Robinson all appeared for Great Britain. But few players ever dominated rugby league like Ellery Hanley did during these decades. Born in Leeds, Hanley rose to fame as a stand-off and in 1985 he became the first player since Billy Boston, and the only non-winger ever, to score 50 tries in a season. Transferring to Wigan in 1985 for a record fee, he switched to loose-forward and captained the club through its glory years. In 1987, the season he scored an incredible 63 tries, he was made Great Britain captain.

Following the 1988 Lions' tour, Hanley stayed in Australia to play for Balmain in the last eight matches of their season, single-handedly guiding them into the play-offs and on to an improbable Grand Final, in which he was deliberately knocked out in the first-half. Without their talisman, Balmain lost, their first defeat since Hanley arrived. His spectacular deeds weren't over though.

In 1991, he moved to Leeds, where despite being the wrong side of 30, he still scored over 100 career tries. In 1995, he replaced Malcolm Reilly as Great Britain coach, the first black person to coach a major British national sports side. Hanley's feats were so immense that if he had played any sport other than rugby league he would have been hailed for what he was – the greatest black British athlete of all time.

These black northerners were complemented by new generations of black Welsh players such as Phil Ford, Gerald Cordle and Ryan Giggs' father Danny Wilson, who continued to go north until rugby union went professional and Welsh selectors dropped their unspoken colour bar.

In the 21st century, the black Welsh tradition was maintained by St Helens' Regan Grace, but most black league players now came from the north's black communities in Leeds, Huddersfield and Manchester.

This is not to say that rugby league was ever free from racism. Despite his star status, Billy Boston often suffered because of the colour of his skin. On the way back from the 1957 World Cup in Australia, Great Britain were scheduled to play exhibition matches in South Africa in an attempt to start the game there. Apartheid laws banned teams in which black and white played together, which meant that Boston would not be allowed to play, stay in the team same hotel or use the same facilities as his white team-mates. However, he returned home early due to a knee injury, according to World Cup team manager Bill Fallowfield, and the issue was avoided. In fact, the injury was exaggerated so that the RFL could send an all-white team, and Billy was left to travel home alone. It wouldn't be the last time he suffered while representing Great Britain. When the 1962 Lions arrived in New Zealand, Billy was detained by immigration authorities. No other player in the squad was questioned and, eventually, the New Zealand government apologised.

In 1988, Des Drummond was left out of the Lions' tour to Australasia after defending himself from a supporter who came on to the pitch shouting racist abuse. Although not on the horrific scale of English soccer, racial abuse of players by spectators was not unknown. In 1978, Doncaster complained about racial taunts towards their black players by opponents. Despite finding this 'unsavoury' the RFL Council decided that this was part of the game and should be treated with 'a low profile'. There were also more subtle signs of prejudice.

Although rugby league gave black players more opportunities than other sports, they were still largely confined to positions that reflected racial stereotypes about speed and strength, rather than in decision-making roles. The vast majority of black players have played in the three-quarters, and especially on the wing, or in the second row of the forwards. The beliefs behind this were articulated by Barry Maranta, former owner of the London Broncos, who said in 1995 that he wanted to recruit local black players: 'They can't play soccer because of their size, but... they're Wendell Sailors. They can sit on the wing and bust through tackles.'

Crowds at rugby league matches have also remained overwhelmingly white, despite the changing demographics of the north. In 1995, researchers from Leeds Metropolitan University discovered there were more black people, 38, playing professional rugby league on one average match day, than the 24 watching it. Despite the sport's strong community focus, its traditional insularity and parochialism have meant there is a glaring lack of engagement with Asian communities in the former textile towns of the north. Only two Asian players, the brothers Ikram and Tony Butt, have played at the highest professional level, with Ikram becoming the first British Asian to play for England in 1995. Three others, Safraz Patel, Gurjinderpal Pahal and Junaid Malik have played international amateur rugby league, while a handful of others, such as Hunslet's Gurdip Singh in the 1970s, Bradford's Abdul Khan and Batley's Saqib Murtza in the 2000s, have signed for professional clubs.

Even with these issues, until the 1980s rugby league stood alone in British sport for its levels of racial equality. The founding principle of the game – that it should be open to all regardless of status – meant that racial prejudice was not as prominent as it was in other sports, and that it could welcome players who would be excluded or restricted in other sports. There were also many people in the game who were

consciously opposed to racial discrimination. When Bill
Fallowfield tried to get rugby league played in apartheid
South Africa in 1957 there was public opposition to it,
articulated by the *Rugby League Gazette*:

> [The South African government's] racial
> discrimination will reap its own whirlwind
> someday. In the meantime, our game should
> confine itself to playing Rugby League. We have
> no colour bar, we judge a man as a man
> irrespective of colour, and anyone good enough
> is eligible to play for the country of his birth. That
> is as it should be, and anyone who tinkers about
> with this in order to 'fit in' with South African
> standards is dealing a death blow at every
> civilised concept of sportsmanship.

Even the *Rugby Leaguer*, a steadfastly apolitical weekly, spoke
out against racist insults shouted at Billy Boston during
Wigan's match against Salford in 1964 (albeit in the language
of the times) arguing that:

> Coloured players, past and present, have brought
> great skill and honour to our game. I hope the
> Wigan winger and his friends will forget this
> incident and remember that the stupid few don't
> talk for all of us. More power to Bill, Roy, Johnny
> Freeman, Colin Dixon and others. We hope they
> will be with us in the RL game for a long time.

This basic belief in equality was common in rugby league's
communities. *Coal is Our Life*, the classic sociological study of
Featherstone in the 1950s, remarked that information '...about

inequality and injustice has a strong appeal to working people; in all sorts of ways these are the marks of their situation in life.' Rugby league accepted as natural black players in positions of prominence and authority as captains and coaches.

For many black players, especially those from Wales, the fact that rugby league was excluded from the establishment and saw itself as an outsider helped to create a common sense of identity. This was captured by Cec Thompson when he recalled the racism he faced as a young man: 'It was bad enough being black ... How much lower down the social scale could one go than be seen as a black, uneducated rugby league player..?' The boyhood lessons learnt by Doug Laughton, the great Widnes coach who signed Martin Offiah, were also taught across tens of thousands of homes across the north of England:

> We never thought that people with different coloured skin were inferior to us. My grandmother used to say: 'There's nobody better than you and there's nobody worse'. The 'nobody worse' bit would prompt me to ask: 'Am I that bad?' I was taught to treat people with respect. We were raised that way even if we never had a great education.

Members of the crowd at Wales v France in 1975

19

•

From the Seventies to Super League

'No club will ever again pay its way through the turnstiles alone'.
— David Oxley, RFL secretary, 1975.

'Last one out, turn the lights off,' said a handwritten sign at the side of the road to the M62 motorway, just beyond Hull's city boundary. On the first weekend of May 1980, tens of thousands of people poured out of the city towards Wembley to attend an historic occasion: Hull FC versus Hull KR in the Challenge Cup final. It was east versus west, red and white versus black and white, freight docks versus fish docks – and the first time that two clubs from a city outside of London had ever clashed in a major rugby or soccer final at the national stadium. A 95,000 crowd attended what could have been billed as the world's biggest private party to see Rovers win by a touch-and-go ten points to five.

Wembley wasn't the first time that season they'd met each other in a final; in December, Hull had edged out Rovers, 13-3, in the BBC2 Floodlit Trophy. The previous season,

Rovers were crowned First Division champions, while Hull topped the Second Division and the age-old rivalry rose to spectacular new levels. The season after Wembley, the clubs clashed again when Rovers took the spoils in the Premiership final while, in 1981-82, Hull got the better of their cross-town rivals in the John Player Special Trophy final. In 1983, the black and whites won the Championship while the red and whites were runners-up, but the next season saw Rovers pip Hull to the title by a single point. In 1984-85, a Peter Sterling-inspired Hull eviscerated Rovers in the Yorkshire Cup final, while his fellow Australian, Gavin Miller, led from the front as Rovers took the John Player Trophy in the last of the great all-Hull finals.

The dominance of the two Hull sides in the 1980s symbolised the old and the new of rugby league. Hull had been a rugby town since the 1860s; the sport was part of the daily warp and weft of its working-class communities. As the city had begun to experience the effects of the loss of many of its traditional industries in the late 1960s, the game had gone into decline. But from the late 1970s, both clubs had spent heavily on building teams that would put them in the spotlight. At first they had signed talented British players like Steve Norton and Phil Hogan, then moved to New Zealand for stars like Gary Kemble and Mark Broadhurst, and then to Australia for icons like Sterling and Miller.

The rivalry between East Hull's KR and West Hull's FC became combustible and provided the fuel for rugby league to gain national prominence. Rarely had two geographic halves of a city become so identified with two teams. Yet the fans who supported Hull and Rovers before rugby's 1895 split would have been most surprised – because in those days Rovers were the pride of West Hull and Hull had risen to prominence as East Hull's team.

*****

Despite Ron Chester's terminal diagnosis in 1970, rugby league was not dead. It was not even sleeping. Despite industrial decline, population movements and changing lifestyles, residual support for the game remained strong. Thanks to the efforts of its supporters and the wider community, Bradford Northern was resurrected after its 1964 collapse and increased its crowds to average over 9,000 by 1968. On the game's biggest stage, the Challenge Cup final at Wembley recorded bigger average attendances in the 1960s and 1970s than in the 1940s or 1950s, hosting capacity crowds three times in the later decades, compared to just once in the post-war years. A turning point for the sport came in 1974 with the retirement of Bill Fallowfield as RFL secretary.

Brian Snape, Salford's entrepreneurial owner and chairman of the RFL, signalled that a change was in the air when he told the press: 'We are an old game and there are too many old men in it. The young men have got to lead the way'.

The young man appointed as the new secretary was David Oxley, the Oxford-educated deputy head of the Duke of York's Royal Military School. Despite his career, the Hull-born Oxley was a rugby league man through and through, and alongside the RFL's first public relations officer, David Howes, he sought to bring the game into the modern world. He embarked on an aggressive campaign to seek out sponsors, a commercial opportunity the RFL had previously let slip through its fingers. It had been one of the first sports to benefit from brewery sponsorship in 1961, when Mackeson Stout awarded gold watches to players scoring the most points against the touring New Zealanders. The following season the Mackeson Trophy was introduced for the season's top-scoring team. In November 1971, the RFL teamed up with cigarette manufacturer John Player and launched the Player's No. 6 Trophy competition, later renamed the John Player Special Trophy.

In same month Oxley took over from Fallowfield, the RFL allowed its clubs to carry advertising on their shirts, something pioneered in the 1960s by French rugby league.

The success of Oxley's strategy could be seen by comparing the RFL's commercial income in the last season of Fallowfield's regime, which totalled just £4,000, and the £28,075 raised by the new administration three seasons later. By 1983, the figure had risen to £413,350, and the game was healthier than it had been since the 1950s. The Challenge Cup final sold out nine times between 1978 and 1995, compared to three times in the previous years since the move to Wembley in 1929. Test matches against Australia attracted unprecedented home crowds, exceeding 50,000 for the first time in 1986 and culminating in the 73,361 who saw the 1992 World Cup final at Wembley. In ten seasons between 1980 and 1995, average crowds for first division matches actually exceeded those in soccer's third and fourth divisions.

On the field, domination by Hull and Hull KR in the late 1970s and early 1980s helped raise the profile of the sport. Both had been aggressively ambitious, regularly breaking the transfer fee record and helping to revive the cosmopolitan glamour of the league in the 1940s, when overseas stars had been great crowd-pullers. Hull's twin sides helped to revive the cosmopolitan glamour of league in the late 1940s, when overseas stars had been great attractors of crowds.

The international transfer ban had been lifted because of the unprecedented impact of the 1982 Australian tour, which saw Great Britain humiliated as never before. Like the England soccer side's loss to Hungary in 1953, the shock at the scale of the 3-0 whitewash – in which Great Britain struggled to score their solitary try – was traumatic and, desperate to learn as much as possible from their conquerors, the RFL called for an end to the international transfer ban. It was lifted in 1983 and 757 Australian players came to play for British clubs over the next decade. Some were among the greatest of all time. As well as Sterling at Hull, blockbusting winger Eric Grothe went to Leeds, Wally Lewis played a ten-match cameo at Wakefield, Mal Meninga won matches and hearts at St Helens, while Brett Kenny and John Ferguson helped to start Wigan on the road to complete domination.

The high point of this invasion was the 1985 Challenge Cup final between Wigan and Hull. It brought the sublime skills of Kenny, Sterling and Ferguson to the attention of a TV audience of millions. Such was the prestige of that generation of Australian players that, in 1990, Mal Meninga went where no other rugby league player had gone before and won the BBC's overseas sports personality of the year award.

This rise in fortunes rekindled long-held hopes that rugby league could break out of its geographical straitjacket and, in September 1980, Fulham became London's first professional rugby league side since Streatham folded in 1937. Bolstered by considerable media interest in the apparently incongruous notion of a 'Northern' sport being played in the metropolis, it averaged crowds over 7,000 and won promotion at the first attempt. However, the club lost £307,000 in its first season and continued to make losses, much to the concern of its parent soccer club. Fulham FC's promotion in 1981-82 eventually led to a loss of interest in rugby league, and less than four years later the club was put into liquidation. Nevertheless, Fulham's initial success led to a wave of soccer clubs expressing an interest in rugby league. Although most never got beyond the idle chatter of soccer's boardrooms, over the next five seasons Carlisle United, Cardiff City, Maidstone United and Mansfield Town either formed their own rugby league sides or were involved in ground-sharing ventures with an expansion side. At the start of the 1985-86 season, rugby league had 36 professional sides, its highest total since 1903.

The game undoubtedly benefited from the crisis confronting soccer in the 1980s. The failures of the national side, declining crowds and, above all, the prevalence of fascistic hooliganism led to widespread disillusionment with the sport. Rugby league was also seen by soccer clubs as a way of boosting income through diversification – '...we want to make some brass,' Fulham soccer chairman Ernie Clay told the press in 1980. But when Clay realised that the league side would not make any, he pulled the plug. Exactly the same happened at Cardiff City and Carlisle United. Of the other clubs who joined the league in the 1980s, only Sheffield survived with any distinction, again thanks to a dedicated band of volunteers and the city's proximity to the game's heartland. As with the greyhound entrepreneurs of the 1930s, the businessmen who set up a rugby league club to make money were always disappointed, because the long-term investment and personal commitment necessary to establish a position in local communities were economically unjustifiable to the mere speculator. Without a broader social commitment to the sport, a professional club couldn't survive.

Indeed, local pride and civic rivalry had been major driving forces behind the two Hull clubs' rise. Fear of being the city's second best led each to deal heavily in the transfer market. In 1978, Hull set a new transfer record when they signed Castleford's Clive Pickerill for £20,000. Over the next two seasons the two clubs leapfrogged each other, setting new high-water marks until Hull KR almost doubled the record in

1981 by paying £72,500 for Wigan full-back George Fairbairn. Wigan's rise from the mid-1980s was also propelled by their transfer dealings. In 1985, they paid £150,000, made up of cash and two other players, for Ellery Hanley, followed by deals of £100,000 or more for Joe Lydon and Andy Gregory. The resulting rise in wages was also fuelled by the influx of players from overseas. Clubs offered premium rates of pay, a trend led by struggling Wakefield Trinity, who paid Wally Lewis £1,300 a match in a vain attempt to avoid relegation in the 1983-84 season. For a four-month stint in England during the Australian close-season, representative players could expect to pick up between £15,000 and £20,000. Naturally, their high wages meant British players demanded their share too.

This spiral was increased by a radical restructuring of the club-player relationship. Traditionally, league used a 'retain and transfer' system based on that of the Football League. Clubs effectively owned their players until they transferred them to another club or the player retired. The system stayed intact until the summer of 1984, when Fulham went into liquidation. Warrington signed two of their leading players, Hussain M'Barki and Steve Diamond, on the not unreasonable basis that as the Fulham club no longer existed, the players could not be under contract to it. However, Fulham was revived by Roy and Barbara Close who claimed the players still belonged to the club. In November 1984, a High Court judge ruled in favour of the players, on the grounds that the new club could not legally own the old club's players registrations.

In response, the RFL introduced a new contract-based system for players in June 1987. A player was now free to arrange a contract with any club he chose but, unlike previously, was not tied indefinitely to that club. A transfer fee would still be payable if the player moved to another club at the end of his contract. It was hoped these reforms would help to curb spiralling transfer fees and allow clubs to control wages more effectively.

In fact, it led to the opposite. Clubs scrambled to offer higher wages to attract players who now had much more bargaining power. Between 1991 and 1994, the sport's gross income increased by three per cent, but expenditure on wages grew by ten per cent. Transfer fees also began to rise rapidly again. In 1987, Leeds paid successive record fees of £150,000 and £155,000 for Hull's Lee Crooks and Garry Schofield. They then raised the bar to £250,000 to bring Ellery Hanley back to his home city from Wigan. This in turn allowed Wigan to pay Widnes £440,000 for Martin Offiah in early 1992. As Maurice Lindsay noted in 1995, with all the wisdom of a sinner turned priest, the contract system had 'caused panic and unrest in the British game' as clubs offered 'ridiculous money for average players. It was the road to ruin.'

It was not the only road to lead to that destination. Clubs also faced the escalating costs of maintaining and improving long-neglected grounds. By the mid-1980s, the former Test match venues of Huddersfield's Fartown and Swinton's Station Road were decaying husks of past grandeur, whose running costs had escalated far beyond their owners' means. This was a widespread issue for almost all stadia, and the consequences of such neglect were horrifically highlighted by the catastrophe at Bradford City's Valley Parade ground on 11 May 1985, which saw 56 people killed. The state of disrepair of the stand which burned down was no worse than at many rugby league grounds.

The Popplewell Inquiry's report into the fire brought the majority of rugby league grounds under the jurisdiction of the 1975 Safety of Sports Grounds Act, which originally applied only to soccer. But most league clubs could not even afford the Act's minimal safety regulations. In the two-and-a-half years after the fire it was estimated that clubs spent over £3 million on ground improvements. It was nowhere near enough to make up for the accumulated decades of disregard.

In 1987, Hull KR, Keighley and Blackpool announced they had to move to new grounds, although Keighley eventually stayed put. York and Rochdale made the same decision the following year. Bradford and Wakefield avoided a similar fate due to local councils buying their grounds. The situation went from bad to worse to calamitous in April 1989 when 96 Liverpool fans were crushed to death at an FA Cup semi-final at Hillsborough. The Taylor Report into the tragedy mandated further ground improvements and the increased expenditure required was enough to capsize a number of clubs. Huddersfield, Swinton and Dewsbury sold their grounds and Blackpool, Bramley, Huyton and the remaining expansion clubs, with the exception of London and Sheffield, eventually collapsed under the burden.

By this time, even unparalleled brilliance on the field was not enough to save clubs from the financial reckoning.

Wigan had been relegated to Division Two in 1980, a humiliating event for a town which was in many ways the embodiment of rugby league. They immediately bounced back and a new board of directors, led by innovative and energetic local bookmaker Maurice Lindsay, rebuilt the club and made it the first full-time professional team, creating one of the greatest sides in the history of the sport. Not since Harold Wagstaff's Huddersfield had one club dominated the game so completely. Like them, Wigan's success was built on stars from Britain, Australia and New Zealand, and was led by some of the greatest players of their times, none more so than Ellery Hanley, as inspirational to his team-mates as Wagstaff had been to his. And where Huddersfield had the try-scoring genius of Albert Rosenfeld, Wigan had Martin Offiah. They were champions for seven consecutive seasons between 1990 and 1996, won the league and cup double six times, and lifted the World Club Championship trophy three times between 1987 and 1994. However, the performance on the pitch wasn't reflected on the balance sheet. In 1993, the club announced a loss of £300,000 on a turnover of £3 million and the following year reported a wage bill in excess of £2 million. But the club's average attendance had plateaued at just over 14,000, while the costs of running such an extraordinary team kept rising. The club also faced the escalating costs of maintaining its Central Park ground, which had been built in 1902.

In fact, all rugby league's dominant sides of the 1980s and 1990s were laid low by the same problems. In 1987, both Hull clubs found themselves in deep crises due to the state of their grounds, and each would eventually leave its traditional home. Widnes, the outstanding team of the mid- to late '80s thanks to an often breathtakingly off-the-cuff style of play coached by the wily Doug Laughton, were confronted with financial meltdown in the midst of the 1992-93 season. Despite the record sale of Offiah to Wigan and a Wembley appearance at the end of the campaign, the problems proved intractable. The club's survival was eventually only ensured by the sale of its ground to the local council and the transfer of the vast majority of its players.

The fact even Wigan could face financial ruin increased the sense of crisis that was enveloping the game and sparked growing calls for radical change. As early as January 1986, Wigan director Jack Robinson had proposed creating a 'Super League' as a way to generate extra television and sponsorship income. It was possibly the first use of the term in rugby league. Robinson was speaking on behalf of a group of twelve of the leading clubs who had banded together to demand a bigger share of the game's revenue and a reduction of first division clubs from 16 to twelve, which of course would consist of themselves.

Rumblings of discontent from the top sides about the financial support given to smaller clubs first emerged in the 1970s. Many leading outfits objected to the fifteen per cent levy on crowd takings, which first division clubs paid into a fund that was distributed equally between all at the end of the season. The levy had been introduced in 1939 and was originally fixed at five per cent, then raised to ten in 1950 and to fifteen, six years later. When two divisions were introduced in 1973, it was decided that only first division clubs should pay it. The top sides increasingly resented it and in 1983 Bradford and Widnes proposed abolishing it. Under pressure from 'Super League' clubs, the RFL reduced the levy to eight per cent in 1986. This was still eight per cent too much for Robinson and his co-thinkers.

The leading clubs now had their eyes on the money starting to come into the game from television rights.

By 1990, matches were on the BBC, Granada, Yorkshire TV, the British Satellite Broadcasting (BSB) network and a short-lived satellite channel for pubs and bars run by British Aerospace. The takeover of BSB by Rupert Murdoch's Sky TV to form BSkyB at the end of 1990 saw league, alongside Scottish soccer, briefly become one of the flagship sports of Sky's as yet under-populated sports channel. The imminent signing of a £3 million deal with Murdoch led to 17 clubs forming a group in early 1992 to demand a larger slice of TV money. In November 1992, Wigan's Maurice Lindsay succeeded David Oxley, another reflection of the increasing dominance of the top clubs.

Under Lindsay, the pace of change quickened.

A committee was set up to look into switching the season to summer, and a plan for the game's development, *Framing the Future*, was published, calling for a 16-team 'Premier League', mergers of clubs, improved stadia and a salary cap, which was endorsed by the clubs in October 1994. Ironically, the major innovator in the sport in the 1990s had been a club outside the elite, Keighley. The town was hit hard by the collapse of the textile industry in the 1970s and, in 1987, the club itself narrowly avoided being wound up by the Inland Revenue. But, in 1991, a group of local businessmen bought the club, renamed it Keighley Cougars and gave match-days a carnival-like atmosphere, with cheerleaders, mascots and loud music borrowed from American football and Australian rugby league, all of which were to become a staple of future Super League matches. Although Keighley adopted the traditional high-risk business model of buying a winning team, they were successful. Crowds jumped to an average of around 5,000. If Wigan led by example on the pitch, the Cougars were the yardstick off it.

In October 1994, the Kangaroos arrived for their 18th tour of Britain, bringing with them not just another Ashes-winning team but also reports of a possible breakaway league in Australia. These speculations added to the febrile atmosphere in the British game, where it was announced in the same month that only four of 16 first division sides had made a profit and that 17 professional clubs were technically insolvent. In December came the jaw-dropping announcement that Jacques Fouroux, a man who symbolised French rugby union in the 1980s, was launching a new summer rugby league competition in France. All of that gave rise to new rumours of major changes in the rugby league world.

It was clear that radical change was coming. But no-one knew how or when.

20

•

Man's Game? Woman's Game!

'It's all about choice. Everyone should have the right to choose what they want to do. We choose to play the sport we love, which just happens to be rugby league. If we are breaking new ground then we're having an awful lot of fun in the process'.
— Jackie Sheldon, GB Lionesses coach, 1996.

The 1970s were the decade in which women's equality came to the fore. The Equal Pay Act of 1970 and the Sex Discrimination Act of 1975 brought legal equality to many aspects of women's lives, and rugby league was not immune.

In 1978, the game made the national headlines when 13-year-old Elisabeth Beal was banned from playing for Normanton amateur rugby league club's U14 team. She was one of at least two girls, the other being Linda Hall, a player with Clayton in Bradford, who were playing in boys' teams that season.

Under public pressure and worried about falling foul of equal opportunity laws, BARLA reversed the ban despite voicing fears about her safety and the possible reluctance of boys to tackle her. BARLA's worries were not shared by Elisabeth, who could now look forward to her next match: 'I expect it will be a hard game. I don't think [boys] would be embarrassed to tackle me – just the opposite. I'm sure they'll try all the harder just to prove a point'.

Stephen Pollard, the Normanton secretary, was firmly on Elisabeth's side, saying 'she can run as fast and tackle as hard as any of them, and as far as the team is concerned, she is just one of the boys.' The founding principle of rugby league was re-emerging as new generations sought equal opportunities.

*****

Although rugby prided itself on being a 'man's game', women were involved in it from the earliest times.

As far back as 1869, newspapers in the north often commented on the presence of women in rugby crowds, and as the sport's popularity increased, so did the number of women spectators. A report of the 1883 Yorkshire versus Cheshire match told its readers: 'Don't imagine that all the spectators were men, for they were not. Indeed, the female element was very largely represented and the comments from this portion of the gathering were as numerous and as critical as those of their brothers, husbands and fathers.' A quarter of the 5,000 people at Manningham's 1884 home match against Hull were reported to be women.

It also seems that women went to matches on their own because, in 1884, Bradford reversed their traditional policy of allowing women free entry to the grandstand.

When Pontefract won the Yorkshire Cup in 1891, it was also noted the crowd which greeted them on their arrival home contained a 'great number of the fair sex. Old girls and new, young and pretty, old and, er, well, er, respected.'

Women supporters were no less committed to the game than men. In 1885, Bradford captain Fred Bonsor received a well-publicised letter from 'young ladies' in Wakefield who accused his club of cowardice for refusing to play Trinity that season. This passion was not confined to younger women either: 'It is somewhat surprising that so many mature matrons patronise the sport, and what is even more surprising is the extent of their knowledge of the game and the pitch of enthusiasm to which they work themselves up,' observed *The Yorkshireman* magazine in 1891. Sometimes women's behaviour at matches did not meet Victorian ideals of womanhood. In 1888, Swinton's chairman criticised female supporters for their 'bad manners and rowdiness'. This rowdiness sometimes went to extreme lengths. When a victorious Batley side left Horbury's ground in 1884, they were pelted with red hot coals by a disappointed female home fan.

Recognising the importance of women to rugby, *The Yorkshireman* protested in 1891 about a 'men only' meeting for Keighley 'comrades'. 'What about the ladies who patronise the Highfield Lane enclosure?' it asked. 'Are they not comrades as well?' However, a significant number of rugby officials did not think they were. Even when investigating accusations of professionalism in rugby, the Reverend Frank Marshall refused to take evidence from women: 'We have no dealings with women here,' he told one woman who claimed to have proof that Wortley FC in Leeds paid its players. One club that certainly did have dealings with women was Broughton Rangers, who were nicknamed 'Mrs Boardman's Boys'. Isabella Boardman was the proprietor of the Bridge Inn, the local pub which served as the club's offices and changing rooms in its early years. She was so closely associated with the side that she became known as the mother of the club, providing moral support, material comfort and, occasionally, financial help to its players.

Despite the high level of interest, there is no record of women playing organised rugby in Victorian times. Although women played in traditional village football matches since at least the early 1700s, modern rugby and soccer officials saw their games as promoting masculine values and eliminating effeminacy in young men, and so barred women from taking part. When women working in munitions factories and other wartime industries tried to take up the game in World War One, men in the sport told them to play soccer as it was seen as a more feminine sport. Women's soccer underwent a boom in popularity, including in many towns where rugby league was the dominant sport such as St Helens, Wigan and Leigh, and it is worth speculating how popular women's league would have become if allowed. Sadly, it would be decades until women's teams finally played rugby league.

In Sydney, the outlook seemed not so bleak. In September 1921, the Metropolitan Blues and Sydney Reds women's rugby league teams played a match in front of over 20,000 people at Sydney's Agricultural Showgrounds, who saw winger Maggie Maloney cross for four tries. But this promising start came to nothing because, despite public support from Dally Messenger and NSW Rugby League secretary Horrie Miller, the league authorities banned any affiliated organisation or individual from involvement in the women's game. Starved of support, the women could not find the resources to continue. In New Zealand that same year, women's sides were formed in the Auckland suburb of Parnell and Hornby, near Christchurch. But, yet again, opposition from league officials snuffed out the movement.

In 1930 there was another attempt in Sydney to organise a women's match, but the officials nipped it in the bud. A charity match took place in Queensland in 1954, but this was never followed up.

Despite being stopped from playing, women remained among the most passionate and committed supporters. In 1930, police escorted a woman from Hunslet's Parkside ground after she rushed onto the pitch to bludgeon Oldham forward Jim Addison with her umbrella. In the 1940s, a St Helens woman supporter became notorious for hitting opposing players over the head as they came out of the players' tunnel. Referee George Phillips claimed in 1954 that 'women spectators are largely to blame' for insulting players and inciting rough play. In 1966, Minnie Cotton of St Helens became a TV sensation when she twice went on the pitch to defend her lodger, Saints forward John Warlow, during a Challenge Cup semi-final and Championship final. Just as important, but far less visible, were the tens of thousands of mothers, wives, sisters and daughters who played an incalculable unpaid role in maintaining and supporting their men's involvement in the game. For a number of players, it was their wives' intelligence and astuteness which enabled them to negotiate careers on and off the field.

Women played an increasingly important role off the field from the 1920s. In schools' rugby league, there was a long tradition of women coaching schoolboys in the game, such as Winnie Powell at Wakefield's St Austin School in the 1940s, and Adriel Collinson at Hunslet Carr school in the 1960s. Women were involved in supporters clubs from the 1920s, and their organisational skills and enthusiasm for voluntary work meant they were crucial to club fundraising and administration for decades. In 1958, Hull's Kay Ibbetson formed what became East Hull amateur rugby league club, which was so successful she organised their pioneering tour of France in 1963. Betty Haile was elected to Whitehaven's board of directors in 1969, the first time a woman had been appointed a club director. In 1984, Barbara Close became the first female chair of a board of directors when she took over at Fulham. That same year, Kath Hetherington became the first woman to sit on the RFL Council when she represented Sheffield Eagles. In the late 1980s, women physiotherapists joined professional clubs, led by Widnes's Viv Gleave. And women also began to make their presence felt on the field as match officials. In 1984, Julie Fitzpatrick became the game's first woman referee when she took up the whistle in the West Yorkshire amateur league and, in 1993-94, Julia Lee became the first woman to officiate at a men's professional match.

By this time, women were breaking down the barriers that prevented them from playing. As Victoria Dawson has uncovered, the first organised women's rugby league matches in Britain took place in 1953 in the Marsh and Quay district of Workington, where three games were organised as part of a carnival to celebrate the Queen's coronation. Marsh Blondes and Quay Brunettes played two matches against each other before combining to become Marsh Hornets in order to play another local team, Dearham Amazons. In front of 2,000 people, the Amazons pulled off a shock 15-6 win. All three matches were taken seriously by players and spectators alike, and were a focus for the local community. Yet despite the athleticism and skills of the players, the matches were belittled by some journalists, an issue that would recur throughout the history of women's rugby.

It was not until the 1970s, when demands for women's equality were felt throughout society, that women began to play league regularly. Elisabeth Beale's inspiring struggle demonstrated the growing demand from women to play the sport. By 1980, there were 'Ladies' clubs at Huddersfield, Leeds and at Pilkington's glassworks in St Helens and in 1986 six sides formed the first women's league, which by 1991 had grown to 18 teams organised in two divisions. The league was strong enough to organise a two-match tour to France in 1989 and, in 1990, Lancashire played Yorkshire at the men's Premiership final at Old Trafford. The game also began to gain a foothold in schools, with ten fielding girls' teams in 1991. The biggest PR boost to the game came in 1993, when Sophie Cox became the first female rugby player to appear at Wembley, running out with the Rochdale town schools' side in the under-11s final before the Wigan versus Widnes Challenge Cup final. Featured on national television news and BBC's *Blue Peter* programme, Sophie had initially been barred from playing by the North-West Counties Schools Rugby League because its constitution declared the game was only for boys. After a public outcry and pressure from the RFL and the English Schools' Rugby League, Sophie was able to take her rightful place in the side and played a key role in Rochdale's 12-6 defeat of Sheffield schools.

In 1996, the game took its biggest step forward when the Women's Amateur Rugby League Association organised the first-ever women's tour of Australia. The Australian Women's Rugby League had been formed in 1993 and the British women were keen to kindle rugby league's traditional Anglo-Australian rivalry. Coached by Jackie Sheldon and jointly captained by Wakefield's Brenda Dobek and Bradford's Lisa McIntosh, who had led the 1989 tour to France, the team had to raise £700 each just to make the tour. There had rarely been money better spent in the game. The Lionesses played a seven-match tour and won a memorable Test series 2-1.

The success of the tour was an example of the way in

which the women's game was taking off around the world. Although women had played it in New Zealand as early as 1966 and in Papua New Guinea in 1976, administrative difficulties and sexist opposition meant that it was not until the late 1990s that governing bodies began to be established. Inspired by this growth, British, Australian and NZ women came together in 2000 to stage the first ever Women's World Cup in England. The inaugural tournament was won by the New Zealand Kiwi Ferns, who defeated England 26-4 in the final. Eight nations played in the next tournament, in 2005, which was again won by the host Kiwi Ferns, who also won in 2008 in Australia. It was only in 2013 that the Australian women began to emulate the dominance of their men and won the World Cup for the first time. They would repeat their triumph in 2017.

Domestically, however, the game suffered from the tremendous changes rugby league underwent in the new century. The switch to a summer season, as in much of amateur rugby league, was not universally welcomed, and much of the work of the 1980s and 1990s was squandered through organisational disputes and lingering male chauvinism among officials. Eventually, in 2014, the RFL set up the Women's Rugby League Championship but, in 2017, a major step forward took place with the creation of the Women's Super League, initially comprised of Bradford Bulls, Castleford Tigers, Featherstone Rovers and Thatto Heath Crusaders. It quickly captured the imagination, attracting record crowds and sponsorship, and in 2020 had grown from the original four clubs to ten.

At last, it seemed that women's rugby league was on its way to fulfilling the potential that its pioneers had seen for it a generation earlier.

21

•

Into the 21st Century

'Rugby league looks simple and so does its history.
Look closer, and one sees a game of endless tactical
complexity and a tradition filled with contradiction'.
— Simon Barnes, *The Times*, 1995.

There were only 14 minutes left of the 2013 Rugby League
World Cup semi-final at Wembley and England were trailing
the world champion New Zealanders, 14-12. England prop
George Burgess was tackled 28 metres out from the New
Zealand posts, and James Roby quickly fed the ball left to
Kevin Sinfield. Sinfield caught Kiwi scrum-half Shaun
Johnson out of position and slipped a short ball to the man
running off his left shoulder, Sam Burgess. Burgess steamed
through the gap, faked to go right, went to his left, ran
through full-back Kevin Locke, and plunged over the line
with Roger Tuivasa-Sheck on his back, to give England the
lead. Sinfield converted to make it 18-14 and an in-control
England were just a dozen minutes from their first World
Cup final in a generation.

But it wasn't to be. With just 22 seconds left in the match, Johnson turned the tables on Sinfield and slipped by him to score the equalising try. With no time remaining, he calmly converted his own effort and took the Kiwis into their second successive final.

It was a match that symbolised just how far the British game had come, but also how much further it had to go to break the dominance of the Southern Hemisphere nations. It also thrust Sam Burgess into the national consciousness for the first time. Televised by the BBC on free-to-air television on a Saturday afternoon, the match was watched by almost three million people and was probably the first league clash ever to trend on the still new Twitter social media network. Burgess was now the face of the game.

Those who had seen him play since he made his debut for Bradford Bulls as a 17-year-old were not surprised; he was arguably the best British forward since Malcolm Reilly. Powerfully-built and prodigiously gifted, he was the rock upon which a winning England side would be built and the fortunes of British rugby league revived. There was only one problem. Sam Burgess, like team-mates Gareth Widdop, James Graham and brother George, played in Australia.

*****

The semi-final was played in an era still defined by a meeting that took place on Saturday 8 April 1995 at Wigan's Central Park. It was there that Britains's professional rugby league clubs voted unanimously to accept BSkyB's then unbelievable offer of £77 million over five years. In exchange, they agreed to create a fourteen-team summer European Super League, consisting of six existing clubs (Bradford, Halifax, Leeds, London, St Helens and Wigan), six merged clubs (Calder,

Cheshire, Cumbria, Humberside, Manchester and South Yorkshire), plus Paris and Toulouse. It was easily the most radical move the sport had ever made, and it took place in the midst of rugby league's centenary.

Although BSkyB's deal appeared to offer a solution to the financial problems confronting the game, its origins had nothing to do with Britain; they were be found 14,000 miles away in Sydney.

From the late 1980s, rugby league had become one of the hottest tickets of Australian broadcasting. The emergence of digital television made it one of the most sought-after commodities, especially for Rupert Murdoch and Kerry Packer who were both seeking to establish pay-TV networks. Sport, declared Murdoch, was the 'battering ram' with which he had established Fox TV in the USA, thanks to buying the NFL, and BSkyB in Britain, where he had scooped up soccer's Premier League. Now it was rugby league's turn.

At the same time, the expansion of the New South Wales Rugby League and its transformation into the Australian Rugby League (ARL) had led to increased friction between the traditional Sydney clubs and its new members.

The most vocal critic was Brisbane Broncos' chief executive, former Australian winger John Ribot, who thought the sport was held back by the self-interest of historic clubs in Sydney's declining population centres. In March 1994, Ribot pitched to Rupert Murdoch the idea of a 'Super League' tailored to the needs of his television network. Murdoch agreed and put the full resources of his News Limited corporation behind it, but the ARL, locked into Kerry Packer's Channel Nine TV network due to an earlier short-sighted decision to give Packer the first call on its pay-TV rights, turned Ribot down flat. In February 1995, Murdoch declared war on the ARL and began to sign players to his new

Super League, largely by the simple method of offering them more money than they had ever seen in their lives.

When Packer responded in kind, Murdoch's men opened a second front in Britain. The ARL had sought to staunch the haemorrhaging by telling players they could never become internationals if they signed for Super League, so Murdoch decided to recruit the other league nations, meaning the ARL would have no-one to play against. For those in any doubt, the subordinate role of the RFL in the unfolding drama confirmed that the balance of power in the game was now wholly in the hands of the Australians.

On the evening of 4 April 1995, RFL chief executive Maurice Lindsay met hurriedly with BSkyB chief executive Sam Chisholm to thrash out a deal. Four days later, the RFL's clubs met in Wigan and voted to accept SkyB's offer. Their eagerness to accept the money outran their common sense, forcing Lindsay to remind them the first rule of negotiation meant they should not accept the first offer. As the *Independent*'s Dave Hadfield reported: 'I have rarely met as dazed a collection of individuals in my life as the chairmen who were hit over the head by the promise of [£77 million] a couple of weeks ago. I believe they would have agreed to anything – indeed several of them voted for things with which, it later emerged, they profoundly disagreed.'

Hadfield was right. The meeting was barely over when Keighley announced they were considering legal action over their exclusion from the new Super League, and the deal quickly began to fall apart. To the complete surprise of officials, the unthinking proposal to merge clubs was met with a storm of supporters' demonstrations and rallies in town centres, at grounds, even on pitches. As an expression of popular opposition to authority, nothing like it had been seen in the north since the 1984-5 miners' strike, a point not lost on the demonstrators: 'They've taken our jobs, now they want to take away our leisure,' one speaker argued at a protest meeting in Wakefield, while another said the problem was that 'this sport always belonged to the working man. Now it belongs to the businessmen.' Under increasing pressure, the clubs began to back away from the original agreement and, with the deal in tatters, a revised Super League plan was issued at the end of April. The mergers and the proposed Toulouse side were abandoned and replaced by a twelve-team league of 1995's top ten first division clubs – Bradford, Castleford, Halifax, Leeds, Oldham, St Helens, Sheffield, Warrington, Wigan and Workington – plus London and a new Paris team. To make things easier, BSkyB raised the amount on offer to £87 million, and eventually, on 29 March 1996, the new summer league kicked-off and rugby league once again entered a brave new world.

When that first Super League season had finished, Wigan for the first time in the 1990s were not the champions, having been pipped by a single point at the top of the league by St Helens. They slipped further back the following season, when Bradford took the title by seven clear points. It wasn't until 1998 that the RFL decided the champions should be decided by an Australian-style Grand Final, which saw Wigan finally win a Super League title with a nail-biting 10-4 win over Leeds in front of over 43,000 people at a rain-sodden Old Trafford. Despite the controversy, divisions and heartache caused by the upheaval, the Super League concept had been vindicated.

This was seen most obviously in rising attendances. In the winter seasons of the early 1990s, the highest seasonal average was 6,511, in 1991-92. This was overtaken in Super League's first season and the average continued to climb until it reached 10,338 in 2008, the highest since the 1950s. Indeed, it was only in 1962-63 and 1988-89 that average attendances had exceeded 7,000 since the 1950s. The average crowd in the second tier, confusingly re-named the First Division, also rose to its highest ever level of 2,531 in 1997, a figure marginally higher than that of the 1962-63 season, when two divisions were introduced for the first time since 1905. However, from 2008 average crowds started to fall. Although in 2012 and 2015 Super League attendances averaged over 10,000, the general trend across the divisions was downwards.

Nevertheless, crowds remained significantly higher than before 1996, not least because a number of clubs – Wigan (in 1999), Hull (2003), Warrington (2004), Salford and St Helens (both 2012) – moved into new stadia and escaped the escalating maintenance costs of an older ground. The switch to summer also played a major role in this; preparing to go to a mid-season match now required little more than changing into a replica shirt instead of wrapping up like Scott of the Antarctic. As was inevitably the case with rugby league, the switch did not meet everyone's approval, with many local leagues affiliated with BARLA (which began a new partnership with the RFL in 2003) opting to continue playing in the winter. Yet despite the huge changes to the game brought about by Super League – no major British sport had ever switched seasons from winter to summer – rugby league essentially stayed the same. It continued to draw the vast majority of its players and supporters from its traditional social and geographical communities, and the way in which it was portrayed in the media did not fundamentally change. Yet this was also true of soccer, rugby union and cricket, all of which went through similar changes at the end of the 20th century, demonstrating that the framework of British sport and its relationship to society had not significantly altered since the outbreak of World War One.

Nor had rugby league's underlying principles changed, despite significant shifts in social attitudes, as reflected when Batley forward Keegan Hirst came out in August 2015. Guarded acknowledgement of homosexual players circulated at least as early as the 1940s, and certainly by the 1980s at least one well-known English player was open within the game about his sexuality. In 1995, Australian prop Ian Roberts became probably the world's highest profile male sportsman to publicly declare he was homosexual. When former Welsh rugby union captain Gareth Thomas switched to league in 2010, just four months after publicly coming out, there was little comment about his sexuality, and when bigots at Castleford started homophobic chants about him during a match, the club was fined £40,000 by the RFL. Hirst came out to virtually unanimous support: 'Changes nowt pal,' was how one fan responded, articulating the game's underlying principle of equality.

As had been the case throughout its history, the game remained acutely affected by changes in the economy. It was not coincidental that Super League crowds began to fall after 2008. This was the year of the global financial crash that saw living standards decline. The impact was felt especially in the north of England, where the effects of de-industrialisation were exacerbated by the government's economic austerity policies. As the *Economist* pointed out in a rare mention of rugby league in November 2013, 'the wealth gap between north and south is growing: between 1997 and 2012 the median wage in Wigan rose by 38 per cent, compared with over 60 per cent in much of London. No wonder league crowds are smaller, ticket prices lower and investors scarcer than in union.'

In 2019, five Super League teams – Huddersfield, Hull FC, Hull Kingston Rovers, Wakefield and Wigan – came from postcodes which were among the ten per cent most impoverished in England, according to the Government's *Index of Multiple Deprivation*. Many other clubs were in the bottom 20 per cent. This meant there was little room to increase the 'average spend per spectator', the classic strategy of sports businesses, nor to boost revenue by increasing the number of events. Indeed, the fact the Challenge Cup final has not sold out once it returned to Wembley in 2007 may be connected to the launch of the multi-match Magic Weekend in the same year, or the attractiveness of an annual trip to the south of France to watch one's team play Catalans Dragons. In tough economic times, the disposable income of even the most ardent rugby league fan became uncomfortably tight.

The most visible example of the economic problems confronting the game was, just as in the 1960s, Bradford. The Bulls dominated the first decade of Super League, winning the title four times between 1997 and 2005, the Challenge Cup twice, and the World Club Challenge in 2002, 2004 and 2006. Powered by a battleship of a pack based on the 'awesome foursome' of props Paul Anderson, Brian McDermott, Stuart Fielden and Joe Vagana, the club dominated the game in a way it had not done since Victorian times. Off the field, the Bulls were the exemplar of Super League's new standards of marketing and public relations – an ambition signalled by its change of name from 'Northern' in 1995 – with average crowds that never dipped below 10,000 before 2008. But the escalating costs of maintaining a champion team, not to mention the financial drain of their dilapidated Odsal stadium, eventually caught up with them. In June 2012, the club went into financial administration, despite fans raising one million pounds in a few weeks to try and keep the Bulls afloat. In 2014, the club once again went into administration and was relegated from Super League. Unable to keep its head above water, the club went into liquidation in January 2017 before, in 2019, being forced to leave Odsal and ignominiously move to Dewsbury.

The game as a whole found it difficult to navigate these turbulent waters. Struggling to attract sponsors, in 2012 the RFL persuaded the Stobart Group to 'sponsor' Super League in exchange for no cash but advertisements on a select number of its fleet of ubiquitous lorries. The deal was cancelled the following year, but a replacement was not found until 2014. Nor was there consistency in the structure of the game. Super League abandoned promotion and relegation in 1998, reintroduced it in 2001 and then discarded it again in 2008, replacing it with a licensing scheme in which clubs had to meet a set of criteria to be eligible to play at the top level.

This was scrapped in 2015 for a convoluted system that saw the season end with Super League's bottom four clubs playing the second tier's top four, to decide which two sides would contest the 'Million Pound Match' to play in the top tier the following season. This was not only complicated, but it also confused 'uncertainty of outcome' – the golden rule of successful sports leagues – with dire mortal peril, as relegated clubs were forced to either abandon most of their playing squad or take a huge financial gamble on immediately bouncing back. To little regret, this cannibalistic system was replaced with single club promotion and relegation for 2019.

To some extent the game had been grappling with these same issues since 1895.

The RFL had sporadically switched between league structures ever since the Northern Union's first season as a single league proved too cumbersome, while promotion and relegation had been a bone of contention even before the split with rugby union. But in the 21st century, despite constant tinkering with promotion and relegation, the real problem lay at the top of the league.

In 25 years of Super League, only Bradford, Leeds, St Helens and Wigan had ever been champions – in fact, by 1998 every Super League champion had already won the title or appeared in the Grand Final. This was in stark contrast to the 25 years before Super League, when thirteen clubs won the title, despite Wigan's dominance from the late-1980s. And in the 22 seasons since the NRL was created in 1998, twelve different teams won its Grand Final. Even soccer's Premier League produced six champions during its first 25 seasons, while Spain's La Liga and Germany's Bundesliga each managed five. Far from ensuring competitive balance in the game, Super League became one of the most uncompetitive leagues in any of the world's codes of football.

Much of the blame lay at the door of the salary cap. Introduced in 1998, the cap initially restricted spending on player salaries to a fixed percentage of a clubs' income, but was later changed to be a flat rate maximum for all clubs, which, by 2019, had risen to £2.1m per season. This was excruciatingly low. The NRL's 2019 salary cap was A$9.6m (approx £5.4m) and the English rugby union premiership's was even higher at £7m. More strikingly, Super League's cap was half that of Wigan's 1996 player budget of £4.2m. League's low salary cap not only meant the British game could not compete with the NRL and retain players like Sam Burgess, but also that it could no longer sign rugby union stars as it had done before 1995, depriving it of one of its most significant recruitment pools.

Most importantly, the low cap meant that it was extremely difficult for ambitious clubs to spend sufficient amounts to attract enough high quality players to challenge the top four consistently. Rather than bringing greater competitive balance, Super League's salary cap helped to lock down its existing inequalities.

Of course, economic realities in northern England severely restricted financial opportunities for the game. One route out of this dilemma was to expand into new territories.

The entry of Catalans Dragons into Super League in 2006 was perhaps the most far-sighted move for the club game since the Cup final moved to Wembley in 1929. The Dragons were created by a merger in 2000 of two of French rugby league's historic clubs, XIII Catalan and AS Saint-Estève, and the region was as much a heartland of the sport as the Heavy Woollen district or the Cumbrian coast. It was these deep roots, alongside the determination of owner Bernard Guasch and the quality of its squads, that led to the success of the Dragons. This contrasted with the two failed attempts at Super League expansion with Gateshead Thunder in 1999 and Celtic Crusaders between 2009 and 2011. Both had the unenviable task of creating a mass spectator sport from a rugby league culture with a very small local base. The Crusaders' hopes were also hit hard by the 2008 crash, which capsized the business of financial backer Leighton Samuels and forced him to leave the club.

The success of the Dragons and the entry of Toronto Wolfpack into the third tier of the British game in 2017 underlined the extent to which all sports were now breaking out of national boundaries.

Ever since modern sport first emerged in the 18th century, its growth has been fuelled by three things: media expansion – whether newspapers, radio, TV or now the internet; advances in transport such as trains, then buses, then cars and now cheap air travel; and increased capital available to watch sport or to invest in it. The revolution in satellite TV and the internet from the 1990s opened a new era for sport and rugby league, despite its almost genetic disposition to parochialism, benefited hugely. When Great Britain won the World Cup in 1972, only four nations competed, the only countries in which the game was then seriously played. In contrast, fourteen nations competed in the 2017 World Cup, another seven playing in the qualifying rounds. For those with long enough memories or sufficient interest, it was also pleasing to see Serbia and Canada, two nations which had played league in the 1950s and 1960s, finally occupying their rightful places in the world game.

The 2017 tournament also underlined the growing importance of diaspora populations to national sides, as Tonga literally came within a fingertip of the final in a heart-stopping semi-final struggle with England. Although league is often portrayed as a geographically limited sport, when the global governing body changed its name to International Rugby League in October 2019 it had 30 members, plus 40 other observer nations. In spite of its more insular impulses, British rugby league could not help but be part of the new globalised sporting world.

And that perhaps is where the next chapter of the story begins. The past 25 years of Super League have been as rich and as compelling as any period in rugby league history, and a glance backwards brings unforgettable images tumbling into memory: the volcanic power of Adrian Morley, the rugged inspiration of Jamie Peacock, the scallywag brilliance of Sean Long, the obsessive-compulsive competitiveness of Kevin Sinfield, the dignified heroism of Steve Prescott and Mike Gregory, Courtney Hill's arcing run to score the match-winning try in the 2019 Women's Challenge Cup final, St Helens' breathtaking 'wide to West moment', Hull FC's breaking of their Wembley hoodoo, Great Britain's carving up the Australians in Sydney in 2006, Warrington Wolves winning the first Physical Disability Grand Final in 2019, Sam Burgess's heroics in 2013 and many more. These are events and this is a sport that deserves the widest possible audience.

Rugby league has yet to find a way of relating to the new world of the 21st century. It has lost many of its inbuilt advantages over the past 60 years. It can no longer financially compete with soccer. The days of rugby union's self-harming amateurism are long gone and the British game is now the junior partner to Australia. Much of its traditional community has been lost due to de-industrialisation or impoverished by the economic system. Virtually all that remains of its original foundations is its commitment to thrilling, wondrous sport and its founding principle of equal opportunity for all. And yet in a world in which entertainment has never been more valuable, and in which equality and diversity have never been more valued, this is perhaps all it needs.

To survive and thrive, it needs to embrace its traditions and make them relevant to new audiences. In contrast to the bland homogeneity of much of the world today, rugby league offers something different. But it always has, ever since players like Teddy Bartram and Dicky Lockwood refused to accept the dictates of rugby union and stood up for what they thought was right. As rugby league's most important journalist of the past 40 years, Dave Hadfield, put it during the game's centenary in 1995:

> There are two sorts of history. There is the history of kings and queens and empires, of church and state and establishment. And there is the history of dissent and subversion, of people who stand up and say, 'No, that's not the way it's going to be'.
>
> As we look for our place in the sun and wrestle for our slice of the corporate cake, we need to

remember that we are part of that latter tradition. We are not quite respectable; there is a hint of the outlaw and the renegade about us. And that, as we start our second century, is not a weakness. If we will but realise it, it is our most enduring source of strength.

Those who gathered at the George Hotel on 29 August 1895 not only created a better game for all to play, but also a sport where openness, inclusivity and creativity carries within itself the hint of a better world for all.

22

•

Further Reading

'There may seem to be little difference between the rugby fan on the terraces at Llanelli and his counterpart at Wigan, but publishers see them quite differently. One reads, they believe, and the other doesn't'.
– Huw Richards, *The Observer* 1987.

Most of *Rugby League: A People's History* is drawn from two academic history books I wrote in 1998 and 2006, *Rugby's Great Split* and *Rugby League in Twentieth Century Britain*, where you can find the references for quotes and other information in this book. For a broader discussion on the evolution of the rugby codes around the world, see my *The Oval World: A Global History of Rugby* (2015), which looks at league and union, and *How Football Began: A Global History of How The World's Football Codes Were Born* (2018), which looks at soccer and the other football games around the world. My *A Social History of English Rugby Union* (2009) also contains much on the codes' common origins and union's attitude to league.

As if to prove London publishers wrong, rugby league books have long since ceased to be rare. The literature of the game has come a long way since Gus Risman's 1958 *Rugby Renegade* (ghost-written by BBC football commentator Kenneth Wolstenholme) became the first book on rugby league to find a national publisher. With specialist UK publishers such as Scratching Shed and London League Publications regularly producing interesting books, there's never been a better time to be a rugby league reader. What follows is a list of titles that relate to the topics discussed in this book, but in no way should be thought to be a complete guide.

When rugby journalist and historian Huw Richards made his comment about publishers there were just two serious historians of the game, Robert Gate and Trevor Delaney. All rugby league historians owe a tremendous debt to Robert and Trevor for paving the way for others to follow. Their books are highly recommended, especially Robert's two volume history of Welsh players in league, *Gone North* (1986) and his history of Anglo-Australian Test matches, *The Struggle for the Ashes* (1986). He has gone on to produce many other books, all of which offer fresh insights into the history of the game. Trevor's books on the origins of the game *The Roots of Rugby League* (1984) and *Rugby Disunion* (1993) broke new ground in the early history of the sport, while his magisterial *The Grounds of Rugby League* (1991) and *The International Grounds of Rugby League* (1995) are still essential, even after 30 years.

For the origins of rugby league, and the other football codes, Graham Williams' 1994 *The Code War: English Football Under the Historical Spotlight* is a truly groundbreaking book that looks at soccer, union and league in the Victorian era. For a richly-illustrated account of rugby league when it was called the Northern Union, look no further than Les Hoole's 2019 *The Northern Rugby Football Union. The Birth of Rugby League, 1895 to 1922*. Graham Morris's biography of James Lomas, *The King of Brilliance* (2010), gives us a fascinating portrait of the life and times of the captain of the first Lions' tour in 1910. Robert Gate and Graham Williams' *A Northern Union Man: The Life of Harold Wagstaff* (2019) is an essential collection of articles that includes Wagstaff's own autobiography.

There are too many club histories to mention individually, but some of the outstanding works include Alex Service's two-volume *Saints in Their Glory* and *The March of the Saints* (1985), Stephen Wild's exhaustive *The Lions of Swinton: Complete History of Swinton* (1999), Brian Heywood's *Standing on the Shoulders of Giants: A History of Rugby League in Huddersfield*, and Roger Pugh's *The Robins: An Official History of Hull Kingston Rovers* (2016). For amateur rugby league, see Graham Chalkley's *Rugby League Back O' T' Wall: The History of Sharlston Rovers ARLFC* (2006) and Graham Williams' *70 Years of Reaching Forward: Shaw Cross Rugby League Club* (2017).

The schools and university games are covered in Phil Caplan and Ron England's *Different Class. The Story of Schools Rugby League* (2012) and Dave Hadfield's *Learning Curve, The Remarkable Story of Student Rugby League* (2013). For a history of the Challenge Cup, Graham Morris's 2009 *Destination Wembley: The History of the Rugby League Challenge Cup Final* is the best yet published, but should also be supplemented by Stuart Sheard's *Making Up The Numbers* (2013), a painstaking account of amateur clubs' long and sometimes controversial participation in the Cup. For a less rigorous, but utterly joyful, approach to the game's heritage, Ken Dalby's histories of Leeds and Headingley are without peer.

On the issue of race in rugby, the 2003 collection I edited with the much missed Phil Melling, *The Glory of Their Times: Crossing The Colour line in Rugby League*, contains chapters on the black pioneers of the sport, from George Bennett to Jason Robinson, alongside a foreword and afterword from Billy Boston and Cec Thompson. Cec's own *Born on the Wrong Side* (1995) is a wonderful work of personal social history, as is Ikram Butt's *Tries and Prejudice: The Autobiography of England's First Muslim Rugby International* (2009). On a broader scale, Ken Thornett's fascinating 1966 autobiography, *Tackling Rugby*, is full of insights into both rugby codes, apartheid, and non-white South African players in British rugby league, a topic that is covered in great detail by *Tries and Conversions: South African Rugby League Players*, Peter Lush and Hendrik Snyders' 2015 deep-dive into the history of South Africans in the game. For race in Australian rugby league, see Joe Gorman's 2019 *Heartland: How Rugby League Explains Queensland*, and for the rise of Pacific Islander players, Patrick Skene's *The Big O: The Life and Times of Olsen Filipaina* (2020) is vital reading.

For the history of women's involvement in the game at all levels, Victoria Dawson's 2017 doctoral thesis *Women and Rugby League: Gender, Class and Community in the North of England 1880-1970* is the definitive work. Ian Roberts' *Finding Out*, the 1997 autobiography of the Australian forward, discusses his experience of being the first openly gay player in the game (and in almost every professional football code). Tony Hannan's classic *Underdogs: Keegan Hirst, Batley and a Year in the Life of a Rugby League Town* (2017) also examines, among many other fascinating topics, the response of the sport to Keegan Hirst's coming out.

Hannan's account of Batley and its community during 2016 is perhaps the most important book published about rugby league in the last decade, combining deep insight into the sport with a fine-grained understanding of the broader social issues facing the post-industrial towns of the north. Dave Hadfield's 2005 *Up and Over: A Trek Through Rugby League Land* provides a similar 'state of the nation' view of the game and its communities from the previous decade. Robert Light's 2010 *No Sand Dunes in Featherstone* uses oral history to look at how the game has responded to sporting and social changes since the 1950s, while Geoffrey Moorhouse's classic *At the George: And Other Essays on Rugby League* (1989) is essential reading on the culture of the game.

Outside of the north, for insights into Wales' relationship with rugby league, Phil Melling's *Man of Amman: The Life of Dai Davies* (1994) is not only the biography of a Welsh rebel who went north in the 1920s and never looked back, but also contains Phil's exploration of rugby league's rebel culture. Peter Lush and Dave Farrar's 1998 *Tries in the Valleys: A History of Rugby League in Wales* remains the best detailed account of the attempts to nurture the game in Wales, while Gareth Williams 1991 *1905 and All That: Essays on Rugby Football, Sport and Welsh Society* gives a broader historical perspective on the social ferment that led to the rise of rugby in the Valleys.

For Australia, the definitive account of game's origins is Sean Fagan's 2006 *The Rugby Rebellion: The Divide of League and Union in Australasia*, while Ian Heads' *True Blue. The Story of NSW Rugby League* (1992) and his *The Kangaroos. The Saga of Rugby League's Great Tours* (1994) are landmarks in its subsequent history. Andrew Moore's *The Mighty Bears! A social history of North Sydney Rugby League* (1996) sets new standards for a club history. For the impact of the Kangaroos, see Mark Flanagan's 2019 *The Invincibles: The Inside Story of the 1982 Kangaroos, the Team That Changed Rugby Forever*.

For New Zealand, the essential books are Bernie Wood and John Coffey's magnificent trilogy published between 2007 and 2009, *The Kiwis: 100 Years of International Rugby League*, *100 Years of Maori Rugby League 1908-2008*, and *Auckland, 100 Years of Rugby League, 1909-2009*. John's 2012 *Strike! The Tour That Died of Shame: The Story of the 1926-7 All Blacks* (2012) is an outstanding account of a rugby league tour. No discussion of books on international rugby league is complete without Gavin Willacy's 2013 account of the 1953 American rugby league pioneers, *No Helmets Required: The Remarkable Story of the American All Stars*.

For French rugby league, go no further than Mike Rylance's 1999 *The Forbidden Game: The Untold Story of French Rugby League* for the birth, rise and banning of the game, and his 2018 *The Struggle and the Daring: The Remaking of French Rugby League* for the story since World War Two. Philip Dine's *French Rugby Football: A Cultural History* (2001) offers a broad history of both codes, while Roger Grime's *When The Cock Crowed* (2015) and *Still Crowing* (2018) provide a fascinating documentary history of les Treizistes.

For the last 30 years of the game, Neil Hanson's *Blood, Mud and Glory. The Inside Story of Wigan's Year* (1991) is one of the best 'fly on the wall' books in any sport, as well as being a warts and all look at one of the great rugby league sides and how they shook up the game. To gain an understanding of the Super League war of the 1990s and its consequences, Mike Colman's *Super League: The Inside Story* (1996) reports the story as it unfolded down under, while Phil Caplan's *Super League: The First Ten Years* (2006) looks at its impact from a British perspective. For the game's complex relationship with the media, Tony Hannan's *Being Eddie Waring* (2008) is essential.

This is not an exhaustive list, even for the topics

covered. Indeed, many aspects of the story of rugby league have yet to be uncovered. For most of the last 125 years, the game's history and culture was largely recorded by word of mouth, with little more than newspaper reports to preserve it. But today, advances in digital technology mean that thousands of newspapers can be searched with a computer, putting history at everyone's fingertips, and the internet means it has never been easier to contact and interview people, opening up new avenues for oral history. If there's never been a better time to be a rugby league reader, today is also certainly the best time to be a rugby league historian.

Timeline

1895: Northern Union founded on 29 August 1895 at Huddersfield's George Hotel. The first season kicks off a week later with 22 clubs.

1896: Bradford's Manningham win the first-ever league championship. NU has 48 clubs at end of season.

1897: Batley win first-ever Challenge Cup. The line-out is abolished, and all goals are reduced to two points while a try remains three points.

1898: Batley Challenge Cup winners again. NU now has 98 teams.

1899: Rules change. When a tackle is completed a scrum is formed.

1900: All-Manchester Challenge Cup final sees Swinton beat Salford 16-8 at Fallowfield stadium.

1901: Bramley's Cumbrian centre Jim Lomas moves to Salford in the game's first £100 transfer deal.

1902: Broughton Rangers become first club to do league and Challenge Cup double after beating Salford in an all-Manchester Championship Final. Rules changed so ball cannot be kicked directly into touch.

1903: NU allows twelve-a-side teams for all non-professional and representative matches, but top flight still plays fifteen-a-side.

1904: The first Northern Union international match is on April 5: Other Nationalities beat England 9-3 at Wigan's Central Park. The match is played twelve-a-side.

1905: George 'Tich' West scores 11 tries and kicks 10 goals to create a new record of 53 points in a game for Hull KR v Brookland Rovers on March 4. The points record is only eclipsed by Chris Thorman in 2011, but the try record still stands.

1906: NU reduces teams to thirteen-a-side and introduces the play-the-ball after a tackle instead of a scrum.

1907: The first-ever RL tourists, Albert Baskerville's New Zealand Professional All Blacks, nicknamed the 'All Golds', arrive in Britain.

1908: First Kangaroo touring team arrives. Albert Goldthorpe's Hunslet become first side to do grand slam of All Four Cups: Championship,

Challenge Cup, Yorkshire League and Yorkshire Cup.

1909: Coventry join the Northern Union, following the six Welsh team which joined in 1908. By 1913 all had folded.

1910: First NU touring team, known as the Lions, visit Australia and New Zealand, captained by Jim Lomas.

1911: Rules updated to mandate all matches 40 minutes each way and numbers have to be worn on shirts.

1912: Lucius Banks signs for Hunslet, the first black professional rugby player and first-ever American rugby league player.

1913: Huddersfield winger Albert Rosenfield scores a still record 80 tries in the 1913-14 season as a key member of Huddersfield's 'Team of All the Talents'.

1914: Harold Wagstaff's British Lions win the Ashes in Sydney with an epic 14-6 Third Test win over Australia, ending the match with just nine fit players.

1915: Huddersfield win All Four Cups, losing two matches all season.

1916: War-time military rugby union team Grove Park ASC win 25 out of 26 matches with team including Huddersfield's Wagstaff, Rosenfeld, Douglas Clark and Ben Gronow, plus two Rochdale and one Oldham player.

1917: Wartime Emergency league is won for second year by Dewsbury.

1918: Barrow pip Dewsbury for Wartime Emergency League title.

1919: Last season of wartime rugby, Emergency League abandoned and Rochdale win Lancashire League. Hull win the Yorkshire League.

1920: John Wilson replaces founding secretary Joe Platt to take charge of the game for the next 25 years. The Lions resume tours down under but Australia wins the Ashes, the last time they would do so for 30 years.

1921: Winger Harold Buck becomes league's first £1,000 transfer, going from Hunslet to Leeds. The Ashes return to Britain after the visiting Kangaroos lose the series 2-1.

1922: At the urging of Australia, the Northern Union changes its name to become the Rugby Football League, and the game gradually becomes known as 'rugby league'.

1923: The Yorkshire Federation of RL Supporters' Clubs is founded.

1924: Wakefield's Jonty Parkin captains the Lions, his first of two tours as skipper, as they retain the Ashes in Australia. British national side, previously known as 'the Northern Union' renamed England.

1925: Jim Sullivan kicks a record 22 goals for Wigan in their Challenge Cup tie with Cumbrian amateur side Flimby and Fothergill.

1926: New Zealand tour Britain for first time since 1907, but tour is a disaster as the Kiwis lose all three Tests and seven players go on strike.

1927: First BBC radio broadcast of a Challenge Cup Final – Swinton versus Oldham.

1928: Swinton become only the third side to win All Four Cups.

1929: The Challenge Cup final moves to Wembley – Wigan defeat Dewsbury 13-2 in front of 41,500.

1930: Britain retain the Ashes in Fourth Test, played after 'Chimpy' Busch is controversially denied a try that would have won the match and the series for the Kangaroos in the 0-0 drawn Third Test.

1931: York play at Wembley in their so far only Challenge Cup final, but lose 22-8 to Halifax.

1932: Australia beat the Lions 15-6 in the 'Battle of Brisbane' which left them with just three forwards, yet the British retain the Ashes with a narrow win in the deciding Third Test in Sydney.

1933: Widnes' Jimmy Hoey plays and scores in every match of their season, first man to achieve the feat.

1934: French international rugby union forward Jean Galia leads the breakaway that establishes rugby league in France.

1935: Wigan stand-off George Bennett becomes the first black international rugby league player when he plays for Wales in their 11-18 loss to France in Bordeaux.

1936: London expansion side Acton & Willesden fold after one season. Sister club Streatham & Mitcham survive one more season.

1937: Jimmy Cumberbatch becomes first black player to play for England in a two-try debut against France. His brother Val plays for England in 1938.

1938: Wales win third consecutive European championship. Hunslet defat Leeds 8-2 in the only all-Leeds Championship final in front of 54,112 at Elland Road.

1939: France win a first European Championship in either code of rugby. New Zealand tour cancelled after just two matches when World War Two breaks out.

1940: England v Wales international at Oldham is interrupted by an air-raid; it restarts when the all-clear is sounded and England triumph 8-5. Bradford win the first of two war-time championships.

1941: Challenge Cup revived and is won 19-2 by Leeds v Halifax in front of 28,500 at Odsal stadium.

1942: Managed by Eddie Waring, Dewsbury win the first of two war-time championships, although their 1943 title is later declared null and void after they are found guilty of fielding ineligible players.

1943: Rugby league established in Canada as the Halifax (Nova Scotia) rugby union switches to league, led by Irish RL pioneer John McCarthy.

1944: Combined Services RL team beats Combined Services RU side 15-10 in a rugby union match.

1945: Cumbria gets first professional rugby club when Workington Town start debut season in the top flight.

1946: British tourists are nicknamed the Indomitables after the aircraft

carrier that takes them to Australia for first post-war tour down under. John Wilson retires as RFL secretary and is replaced by Bill Fallowfield.
1947: New Zealand tour Britain erasing memories of 1926 and 1939. British national side changes name from England to Great Britain.
1948: Wembley is sold-out for first time as Wigan beat Bradford 8-3 in the Challenge Cup Final.
1949: Australia join International Board created in 1948, after an aborted attempt to create an Imperial RL Council in 1927.
1950: Australia win Ashes for first time since 1920 when Ron Roberts scores decisive try to give them 5-2 win in third and deciding test.
1951: Captained by Puig Aubert, France make their first tour of Australia and win the test series 2-1 playing mesmerising rugby.
1952: Workington win Challenge Cup, the first time the trophy goes to Cumbria; the previous season Town had won the Championship for their one and only time.
1953: Women living in the Marsh and Quay area of Workington play Britain's first-ever organised games of women's rugby league.
1954: The inaugural Rugby League World Cup is played in France and unexpectedly won by Great Britain who defeat the hosts 16-12 in the final. Warrington defeat Halifax in the Challenge Cup final replay in front of 102,575 at Odsal stadium.

1955: Blackpool Borough complete their first season as a professional club. They last until 1987.
1956: Hull win the Championship, coached by Roy Francis, the first black professional coach in any sport in the UK.
1957: Australia win the first World Cup tournament to be played in Australia. No final played as title is decided by a league of Australia, France, GB and New Zealand.
1958: Alan Prescott plays for 78 minutes of Second Test in Brisbane with broken arm, one of five badly injured British players in team that still beats the Australians, 25-18.
1959: Ike Southward moves from Workington to Oldham in the first £10,000 transfer.
1960: David Storey's classic novel *This Sporting Life* published to wide acclaim. Film adaptation is released in 1963. Great Britain win the World Cup, which they host for first time.
1961: Featherstone propose move to summer. Leeds win Championship for first time, beating Warrington 25-10 in the final.
1962: Two divisions replace single league structure for first time since 1902. The 1902 experiment lasted three seasons; this lasts just two.
1963: Kangaroo tourists take back the Ashes, winning first two tests by stunning 28-2 and 50-12 scorelines.
1964: Substitutes allowed for first time, one year before soccer.
1965: BBC2 Floodlit Trophy starts,

initiative of new channel's controller David Attenborough, and lasts until 1979. Castleford are first winners.

1966: Unlimited-tackle rugby ends and is replaced by four tackles, which is raised to six in 1972.

1967: Wakefield win their first ever championship, beating St Helens 21-9 in a replay after drawing 7-7.

1968: Leeds beat Wakefield 11-10 in 'Watersplash' Challenge Cup final. Don Fox wins Lance Todd Trophy for player of the match but misses a last-minute conversion to win cup.

1969: Betty Haile becomes a director of Whitehaven, the first woman director of a rugby league club.

1970: Great Britain win Ashes series for the (so far) last time by winning the final two tests in Sydney.

1971: Cigarette manufacturer John Player sponsors new mid-season trophy, known as the Player's No. 6 Trophy (1971-77), John Player Trophy (1977-83) John Player Special Trophy (1983-89) and the Regal Trophy (1989-96).

1972: GB win the Rugby League World Cup in France, captained by Clive Sullivan the first black athlete to captain a British national side.

1973: Two divisions reintroduced for third time, ditching the single league format for the last time. BARLA formed in Huddersfield.

1974: Drop goals reduced from two points to one. David Oxley replaces Bill Fallowfield as RFL secretary.

1975: Australia crowned world champions after a 'World Series' tournament played between May and November in Australia, New Zealand, England and France.

1976: Great Britain international Phil Lowe scores decisive Manly try in their 13-10 Grand Final victory over Parramatta, underlining the influence of the 'British' invasion of Sydney in the 1960s and '70s.

1977: Man of Steel award for player of the season starts. The inaugural winner is Leeds hooker David Ward.

1978: The Kangaroos retain the Ashes in England, but lose the test series with France 2-0.

1979: Neil Fox retires after 25 seasons with a world record 6,220 career points.

1980: Hull KR defeat Hull FC 10-5 in the Challenge Cup Final at Wembley. Fulham start their first season in Division Two, the first professional London side since Streatham & Mitcham in 1937.

1981: Wigan are runners-up in Division Two and are promoted after their only season ever outside the top flight.

1982: The Kangaroos beat Great Britain 3-0, are dubbed 'The Invincibles' and change RL forever.

1983: Value of try increased to four points, handover rather than a scrum after six tackles introduced, and sin-bin is brought in.

1984: Great Britain lose both test series, 3-0, in Australia and New Zealand. Barbara Close first woman to chair a professional rugby or football club board of directors when she takes over at Fulham.

1985: Wigan defeat Hull 28-24 in a Wembley Cup Final hailed as the greatest of all time. Ellery Hanley becomes first player to score 50 tries in a season since Billy Boston in '62.

1986: Joe Lydon moves from Widnes to Wigan in rugby league's first £100,000 transfer.

1987: British champions Wigan beat Australian champions Manly 8-2 in a World Club Challenge in front of 36,895 at Central Park.

1988: Great Britain defeat Australia 26-12 in the Third Test in Sydney, their first win since 1978 and first in Sydney since 1974. RFL opens its Hall of Fame to honour the immortals of the sport.

1989: Welsh rugby union captain Jonathan Davies signs for Widnes, one of four stellar signings to switch codes to league that season.

1990: Wigan win the league and cup double for first of six consecutive occasions. Rugby league kicks off in Russia, Moscow Magicians making first-ever Russian tour of England.

1991: Three Divisions introduced for first time. Blood-bin brought in.

1992: Maurice Lindsay replaces David Oxley as RFL chief executive. Rules changed so defenders have to be ten metres from the play-the-ball.

1993: Lancashire and Yorkshire Cups played for last time in 1992-93 season, both having begun in 1905.

1994: Ellery Hanley appointed Great Britain coach, the first black coach of any British national team, but Kangaroos win test series 2-1.

1995: Last season of winter rugby league. The biggest World Cup so far is staged in England and Wales and features ten teams.

1996: Summer Super League begins.

1997: World Club Championship between British and Australian Super League sides; Australian sides win all but eight of 60 pool matches and Brisbane win title.

1998: Sheffield Eagles beat Wigan 17-8 in one of Wembley's biggest-ever shocks in a Challenge Cup final. Grand Final introduced to decide Super League champions, returning to the tradition of Championship play-offs.

1999: Rules changed to introduce 40-20 kick. Gateshead Thunder play one season in Super League before merger with Hull.

2000: Australia wins the World Cup, the first to feature 16 nations.

2001: Kangaroos tour Britain for first time since 1994, winning series 2-1. Challenge Cup final played at Twickenham for the first time.

2002: Strella Kazan become first Russian club to play in Challenge Cup, losing 20-16 to Hull amateur side Embassy

2003: Kangaroos tour Britain and win all three test matches by coming from behind in the last few minutes of each game.

2004: Jamaican RL Board founded and joins RL European Federation established the previous year.

2005: Challenge Cup final moves from traditional first week in May to August Bank Holiday weekend.

2006: Perpignan's Catalans Dragons join Super League.

2007: Challenge Cup Final returns to Wembley. Magic Weekend starts. Great Britain plays its last home test series, a 3-0 win over New Zealand.

2008: New Zealand win the World Cup with an unexpected 34-20 final victory over hosts Australia.

2009: Licensing introduced for Super League clubs and promotion and relegation abolished. Wales's Celtic Crusaders join Super League.

2010: NRL changes rules so corner posts no longer touch-in-goal for player in possession of ball. Super League introduces this rule in 2012.

2011: Celtic Crusaders withdraw from Super League.

2012: St Helens move to Langtree Park after 120 years at Knowsley Road, joining Wigan, Warrington, Widnes, Hull, Huddersfield and Salford in stadia built since 1994.

2013: Most successful World Cup ever is staged in Britain, Ireland and France. England miss final after last-minute Shaun Johnson try for New Zealand, who then lose to Australia.

2014: Women's Rugby League Championship starts and becomes Women's Super League in 2017.

2015: Licensing for Super League clubs abolished and promotion and relegation re-introduced via mini-league of bottom four Super League and top four Championship clubs in Qualifiers known as the '8s'

2016: Thatto Heath Crusaders win their fourth consecutive Women's Challenge Cup.

2017: Tonga just miss out on the Rugby League World Cup final when they lose by two points to England in a nail-biting semi-final.

2018: Catalans Dragons win the Challenge Cup, first time a team from outside northern England has claimed the trophy.

2019: Canada's Toronto Wolfpack are promoted to Super League after starting in League 1 in 2017.

2020: Rugby league halted in both hemispheres as result of coronavirus pandemic. The NRL returns first on May 28, Super League following on August 2, both behind closed doors.

Discover more about the history of rugby league with Tony Collins at www.rugbyreloaded.com